DATE DUE

DEC 2 2 2009	
JUN 1 4 2010	
FEB 8 2012	
RENEWED 2/29/12	
MAR 2 8 2012	
JUN 19, 2015	

DEMCO, INC. 38-2931

Hugging Life

A Practical Guide to Artful Hugging

Martin Neufeld
The Hugger Busker

Published by the Author
Montreal, Canada

Editor: Andrea Zanin
Book Design: Samantha Wexler
Book Layout: Richard Strother
Cover Art Photos: François Miron
Back Cover Flap Photo: Yanick Macdonald

Illustrations: Copyright 2006 Leanne Franson

Library and Archives Canada Cataloguing-in-Publication
Neufeld, Martin, - Hugging life : a practical guide to
artful hugging / Martin Neufeld, the hugger busker.
1. Hugging. I. Title.
BF637.H83N49 2006 158.1
C2006-901501-5

ISBN 0-9780599-0-5

Published by the author
Printed and bound in Canada
on 100% recycled paper

WORDS of WELCOME

This book is neither story, nor study, nor thesis, nor manifesto. It is a journey of human tenderness revealed one hug at a time.

I would not suggest reading all the hugs described in my Treasury of Hugs straight through, but rather, take the time to explore them in a haphazard way. Hugs are like the finest chocolate truffles; they are best when savoured lovingly one at a time, in nibbles and bites, so that their richness does not overwhelm the senses.

It is in this spirit that I invite you to wander leisurely through these pages and discover what is possible when you choose to embrace others with your life.

This book is inspired by my mother's profoundly loving and spiritual nature and is dedicated to all those who have forgotten that unconditional love and the kindness of comfort are just a hug away.

WORDS of GRATITUDE

To you who have

Loved me unconditionally though
I was blind to your gift

Shared your light when
darkness would overwhelm me

Touched me deeply when
I could no longer feel myself

Offered me your wisdom when
ignorance was my companion

Taught me by your authenticity
how to be true to myself

Inspired, guided, and supported me in the
advancement of living kindness and
the beauty of hugging

My parents Peter and Theresa Neufeld; my sister
Annik; my partner Jade Chabot; my guides, friends,
supporters and fellow huggers Caitriona Reed,
Michele Benzamin-Miki, Andrea Zanin, Richard
Strother, Samantha Wexler, Peter Snow, Maurice
Taylor, Seana McGee, Sabrina Defeyter, Vivian
Battah, Elysa Battah, Stephen Adams, Sue Medleg,
Magali Jolander, Arden Ryshpan, Marc Dfouni,
Fady Atallah, Ralph Dfouni, Marian Kolev, Kevin
Lo, Yan and Bo Huang, Stan J. Rog, Jean-François
Pichette, Ivy O'Reilly, Mary Stark, Michel Laprise,
Mary Deros, Manuel and Jean-François Fraia, Heba
Aly, Peter Anthony Holder, Brian Britt, Dominic
Papineau, Luc Simard, Deena Aziz, Michael Rudder,
David Roffey, John Peel, Valerie Houston, Maître
Jacques Lecoq, Rodney Cottier, Pamela Barnard,
Mireille la Merveille, the happy-go-lucky one-legged
cyclist, his mother, and the thousands of other
amazing beings who have showered me with their
hugs, gifts, kindness and love.

To all who have journeyed with me and
who continue to do so
I offer you my deepest gratitude and
endless heartfelt hugs.
I thank God for the wonder that is my life and
for the opportunity to live it once again.

CONTENTS

Sometimes it is good to begin with a hug,

because every hug invites a happy ending!

- 1 -

A HUGGER'S JOURNEY

"While visiting Montreal this past August I experienced something new. I walked the square in Old Montreal with my girlfriend. As we watched magicians perform, we kept walking past this statuesque man hugging people. My girlfriend kept saying that she wanted to hug him, and being sceptical I warned her of the possibility of the hugger being a pickpocket. We must have passed the Hugger Busker six times and each time I watched with an untrusting eye. On our last day in Montreal my girlfriend asked if we could stop in the square so she could 'hug the hugger.' She was afraid she would regret not taking full advantage of our vacation. We went to the square and he was there again. She hugged the hugger and she asked me if I had money for a tip. I reached into my wallet and the hugger approached me and asked, 'May I hug you as well?' I reluctantly agreed—and it was the most comforting hug I've ever had in my life.

I still think about it from time to time (five months later) and we are planning another trip back to Montreal next year for another hug. We describe to our friends the ability you had to brighten our day; since then we spend our time thinking of ways to brighten other people's days. That one hug was our inspiration to make the world a little better. Please don't stop hugging; you are making a difference in direct and indirect ways.

Thanks for turning a sceptic into a philanthropist."

- Eric R., Pennsylvania, USA

This testimonial and all other testimonials in this book are taken from the guestbook at www.huggerbusker.com.

The Journey Begins

I am a performer. I believe that my role as a performer in society is to be a social catalyst in which human nature, in all its shades and hues, can be brought to light; I want to stimulate reflection, action and change within individuals and society as a whole. I am an artist, and I aspire to express my life's wisdom through my art, and to create art out of my life. I am a man who, through the grace of God, has been offered a second chance to transform my life from one of despondent emptiness and bitter regret into a truly meaningful and edifying journey. First I went through humility, then surrender, then acceptance, then courage... and finally the inspiration that showed me the beauty, the power and the wisdom of unconditional loving kindness.

In over two decades of performing in film, television, and theatre, I rarely felt that my so-called vocation affected people in the positive ways that I had aspired to. All too often, the roles offered to me were of an intense and disturbing nature. I became so proficient at expressing the dark side of humanity that it became my calling card. Over time this darkness entered my personal life and I felt divided from within. The growing conflict between my ideals and the way I made a living created constant turmoil in my mind and heart. To others I seemed successful, confident and peaceful, yet dissatisfaction and emptiness had become my constant companions. As I was marinating in the bitterness of a divided whole, a deep sense of grief engulfed me until I could no longer escape the reality of the life I'd created.

For years I drifted aimlessly, stewing in my dissatisfaction and floating from one mediocre project to the next, from one heartbreaking relationship to another. I was truly lost to myself, and as a result my potential as an artist, as a partner, and as a human being remained unfulfilled. It angered me that with each passing day I became more and more miserable because I felt helpless to change my situation. Though the desire for deeper meaning and purpose burned strongly within my heart, I could not for the life of me figure out what to do about it.

I am not one to cry in my soup; rather I try to make do with what I have in the best way I can. Still, there were days when the mask of civility would crack and I would weep uncontrollably, or vent my rage. It became habitual for me to throw my bicycle at cars that had cut me off. I hated the anger that would possess me. I even began to fear it. It was hard to accept myself as an unhappy, angry person, but I knew that if I didn't change my ways I would end up in the hospital, in jail, in an institution or all three. I also had to accept that my state of being was the direct cause of the events in my life. I was calling forth into my daily life situations and people that reflected what I was living within: disharmony, grief, fear, anger and helplessness.

The First Step

The first step towards changing the condition of my life was when I chose to take full responsibility for it. I realized one morning, while I slowly pedaled home after an angry incident, that I just couldn't spend my life throwing my bicycle at cars. The anger I was feeling had nothing to do with the cars or the drivers, but my unhappiness with my life. If I wanted things to change in my life, I had to make those changes myself. Releasing myself from blame and guilt, I could then begin to search within for the source of my anger.

What emerged was this: I realized that I had still not come to terms with a traumatic yet amazing near-death experience I had as a young boy. My life was almost stolen from me one day when someone tried to drown me. and the repercussions of that fateful afternoon continue to affect the course of my life. In that moment of forced surrender I was plucked from the confines of my body and lifted into a universe of brilliant light. A luminescent aura of soothing comfort washed away all my trauma, fear and need, replacing all my desire with a sense of blissful contentment in simply being that to this day remains indelibly etched into the core of my soul. Enveloped in this Divine light, I knew that I had come home, as I felt myself entering the presence of God and transforming into love and light. I floated in the lush silence of complete understanding. But my time had not yet come, and my spirit spiralled back into my small and frightened body.

From that moment onwards, I desperately wanted to return home to this Divine all-embracing illumination. Decades later this longing for home still burned fiercely. It led me to a dark, dank dungeon deep within myself, where I staggered about, shackled in self-pity and dejection. Though blinded by darkness, I persisted in my search for a way out. Over a period of years, I tried many different means to heal—various therapies, life-affirming books, spiritual guidance, sensorial explorations, meditation retreats, solitude, hedonism—anything that I thought might help ease the suffering. Slowly I began to see a glimmer of light, and it showed me the truth of my reality. I realized instead of seeking the answers outside of me I needed to look within myself to find them. Before any meaningful change could take place I had to take full responsibility for my life. But how? What did that responsibility entail? I needed not just to change my life, but to completely restructure it, re-evaluate my priorities, rekindle my faith in spirit and myself and then actively live by that faith. It became clear to me that I had to fully merge my performance work, my personal convictions and my spiritual evolution into a seamless whole if I was to ever find harmony and happiness in my life.

It took me thirty-five years to come to terms with being returned to my flesh once having touched the Divine—to realize that I was not rejected by God and cursed to live in a hungry, needy, decaying body, but rather blessed with a gift of understanding, compassion and a deep capacity to love. It was meaning and purpose that I most needed to find in my life, and through the grace of God, meaningful purpose found me in a most auspicious fashion: while I was standing in the middle of a public square.

The Public Square

In 2004, the film industry in my town had all but shut down and I was a hungry actor looking for a paying audience—hungry for attention, for inspiration, for a way to make a decent living in a fun and creative fashion. I had worked steadily as an actor for over twenty years and I wasn't about to let a slump in the entertainment industry burst my bubble. So I decided it was time to go out and make my own work, create my own art.

Early that year my partner, Jade, brought to my attention an international call to audition for Cirque du Soleil. Though I had spent several years training under one of the great physical theatre masters of Europe, the late Jacques Lecoq, I was reluctant to audition—it meant going into an intensive few months of preparation and training and I didn't know if I was up to it. Today I am extremely grateful that I gave in under Jade's gentle insistence. Once I got started, my passion for the language of physical expression very quickly returned. I found myself inspired, and I developed many strange and amusing characters.

My presentation to Cirque was very well received, but I did not find a place in their wonderful world. Nonetheless, the experience itself opened me to a whole other world: that of street performance, which is where Cirque du Soleil finds its own roots.

The day after the audition, I purchased a performance permit from the City of Montreal, and without further ado, I launched myself into the unknown. Attracted by the style and elegance of the 1900s, I put on an old bottle-green linen suit, a high-collared cream shirt, a tan vest, a silk tie and wingtip shoes. I stuck a yellow flower in my lapel, and a bright green fedora topped off my look. To my nameless character, I added three personal elements. First, I wore my grandfather's gold ring, shaped like two hands holding a ruby-coloured stone—a reminder that only I hold my heart in my hands. Second, I wrapped my Tibetan buffalo-bone mala (Buddhist prayer beads) around my wrist to remind me that every moment of my life is sacred and precious and deserves to be honoured with mindfulness and compassion. The last item was a beautiful rosewood rosary that my mother had given me. This I placed around my neck as a reminder that the power of my inner Christ's unconditional love and forgiveness lay in my heart.

Picking up an angel-motif umbrella and a battered leather suitcase, I tucked my creative courage under my arm and headed down the cobbled streets of Old Montreal towards my destiny.

Performing on the streets was new to me, and my intention was to revisit some of the quirky character-driven physical theatre skits that I had developed over the years and had just recently presented to Cirque du Soleil. I was hoping that the public would be enthralled enough by my unusual spectacle to drop a dollar or two into my hat. Still, I wanted to do more than entertain. I wanted to challenge my audience, to push the envelope by giving them performance art that was not only thought-provoking but emotionally stirring as well.

I had never worked the street before and I was scared. Scared of failure, scared of humiliation... basically, scared of falling flat on my face in front of a demanding crowd and going home penniless. One needs courage, stamina and a very thick skin to be a street performer, a busker. Playful, engaging and absolutely genuine is what I needed to be if I was to offer intelligent, original and captivating amusement. It has always been difficult for me to bring the child out in myself. I can at times be very shy but I had to face my resistance and my fears in order to be the loving, happy child that I once was and to perform from the heart.

I made my way to the large public square in the old city. The square was ringed with quaint outdoor cafes, galleries and shops, and was crowded with locals, tourists, caricaturists, painters, musicians and buskers of all stripes. With patience I found a little place at the top of the hill where I could set down my case and ply my brand of entertainment.

I stood there not quite knowing how to start, how to entice the crowd to stop, how to keep them watching, how to ask for money. How on earth did buskers do all that? All these questions and so many more flowed into my mind until I was drowning in uncertainty and insecurity. People would stop and look at me wondering what I was up to. I could see the desire for entertainment in their eyes as they watched me expectantly, but I just froze up. I paced up and down for an hour or two trying to pluck up my courage but to no avail. Day after day I went to my spot on the square ready to play, but each time I left soon after with my tail firmly tucked between my legs.

I was frustrated and disappointed with myself for being so self-conscious and insecure. I was a seasoned performer, damn it! This should have been a walk in the park for me, but it wasn't. I had discovered that the street is a playing field with its own harsh rules, and like the gladiators of old, it's the audience who decides on the spot, with a thumbs up or thumbs down, whether you survive or die. I was dying a thousand deaths and I hadn't even begun.

Losing My Courage, Finding My Hugs

A week later I was confiding my frustration to my sister, Annik, and telling her about my lack of courage. As if it was the most obvious thing, she said, "Why don't you write a sign that says 'I have lost my courage!' and sit on your suitcase and wait for something to happen? If you are patient something *will* happen." It was a stroke of inspired genius. Excited, I hugged her in thanks and dashed out. That afternoon I returned to the square armed with vigour, inspiration and a small chalkboard. For the rest of the day I sat on my suitcase in total stillness, like a living statue, next to a sign that proclaimed my loss of courage.

People were enthralled at the boldness of my action, or rather inaction. I, in turn, was amazed by their reactions. They stopped; they stared; they came to talk to me to encourage me, to offer advice or concern. Some even left money in my tin and when they did I silently thanked them and shifted into another suitable pose.

I realized that just being present in stillness was entertaining, and that the context of my living tableau touched people. Many seemed to recognize themselves in my state of lonely solitude. Every day I returned with a new comment for my chalkboard and a little more courage in my heart. Slowly I worked my way from immobility to active performance, doing situational improvisations with whoever walked by. Every once in a while I'd attempt a short skit. I was beginning to have a lot of fun, as more and more people would stick around to enjoy my playful madness. That's what it was—silly, uninhibited madness. And it seemed to amuse and fascinate people. At times when shyness or insecurity overcame me, I simply retreated back into another pose of silent stillness.

As each day passed my confidence grew, and I found myself more and more receptive to inspiration. I was becoming a welcome divertissement as people came by day after day to read what I had written on my board and see what quirky amusement I had to offer. Then one sunny morning as I strolled up to the square, I noticed a restaurant chalkboard advertising the establishment's special of the day. I thought nothing of it until I was getting ready to write something inspirational or witty on my board. Then it struck me: I could offer my own special of the day! But what? On a whim, I thought about hugs. I love hugging my friends, hugs make people feel good, and they are free. So "Free Hugs"—that would be my special treat today.

I hadn't thought about the consequences of my proposition, or considered whether I was even capable of hugging any and every person who wanted me to. It just seemed like the perfect thing for me to do at the time, and looking back today I know it was.

The response was instantaneous. People just stopped in their tracks! They seemed dumbfounded, surprised, amused, even amazed by the sight of an elegantly dressed man standing in absolute stillness, with arms open wide, offering free hugs. Some would approach slowly to peer at me and see if I was for real. Others would stay back, hoping for someone else to venture forth. The more courageous—or were they foolhardy?—took a trusting leap into my waiting arms. Those who indulged were gratified and pleasantly surprised by the genuineness of my embrace. Almost everyone who walked by, whether they came for a hug or just watched from a distance, left with a cheerful smile on their face and a bit of lightness in their heart.

Over the next few weeks it became clear to me that giving hugs was bringing the public much more than light entertainment; my actions were affecting their inner state in very positive ways. Witnessing the appreciative smiles, the hearty laughter, the expressions of joyful wonder and the sparkle of delight that shone in people's eyes brought me a happiness I had rarely experienced as a performer. Until then I hadn't realized that bringing pleasure to others would bring me such pleasure in return. From then onwards, "Free Hugs" became the heart of my performance.

Within a month I was hugging several hundred people a day, all day, every day. So many people wanted to know my name, who I was and why I was hugging strangers, that I decided to create a web presence that would satisfy people's growing curiosity. Jade, in all her intuitive wisdom, suggested a great name for my character and website. It was simple, she said: I was someone who hugs, so a hugger, and I was someone who performs on the street, so a busker. Thus the Hugger Busker was born! His mission was to be a charming and cheerful provider of heartfelt hugs. The name and the site turned out to be an excellent decision because they gave me a verifiable identity that legitimized what I did. I was constantly dealing with the mistrust people feel towards friendly strangers, especially if they are offering something as intimate as a hug, so a touch of legitimacy helped. It was also an apt way for me to document my adventures as a public hugger by creating a journal and posting photos and testimonials.

"You are such a true inspiration, and made a huge impact on our group, which was in Montreal this week on a mission trip. As great as it feels to serve, you were definitely the highlight of my trip, and I know you made a huge impact on one of my youths. The rest of the trip, she had a huge glow about her, and couldn't stop talking about your hug. We hadn't really realized until then how emotional a person she was. You not only changed her, but you changed the rest of our group through her, as well as through your wonderful, real hugs."
- Krystal S., Kansas, USA

Learning to Smile

Since the beginning of this adventure I have tried to let myself be inspired and guided by people and events around me. The guestbook on my website has been inspirational to me. Whenever I get discouraged, I go online and read the testimonials that people from around the world have written. Some comments move me to tears, some move me to laughter, but they all move me to continue hugging.

Once a man walked by and noticed that I was looking rather pensive. He said to me, "You look too serious, you should smile." I took his word for it and began to do so. Another time a girl told me that I looked tired and should take a break, but not to worry, she would give out hugs for me. I took her up on her offer and lay down on a grassy knoll nearby for a short nap while she delighted in giving hugs. I returned to my hugging rested and energized, and she left happy, grinning from ear to ear. These experiences, and countless others like them, have shown me that the people who cross my path are messengers sent to guide me, if I will only listen.

Standing in stillness and silence all day, in between hugs, was not as difficult to do as people might assume. My years of meditation, martial arts, yoga, and mindfulness practice gave me the physical stamina, the emotional temperament and the inner presence to connect with the grounding force of Mother Earth. My breath became my source of strength and stillness, my stillness brought me silence, and my silence opened my heart to the loving presence of God within me.

This was the first time in my career that my performance work merged seamlessly with my spiritual practice and personal aspirations. Since I began exploring mindfulness and loving kindness meditation in the mid-90s, I've taken up the challenge to incorporate it into both my personal life and my working life.

I am not a religious person; I don't follow any specific dogma or dictates. I am, however, a deeply spiritual man. I believe that within each of us lays the essence of a loving compassionate God, the source of all our goodness and abundance, and that for us to evolve as emotional and spiritual beings we must honour this Divine force by seeking out its wisdom and surrendering to it, so that the light of love and kindness is reflected in our every thought, word and deed. And I certainly have had the chance to put my belief into practice!

There was more to my act then even I realized. The countless hours I spent sharing heartfelt hugs were directly affecting my inner life. I had begun the summer as an out-of-work actor turned busker to make ends meet, as a man with sadness and bitterness lodged deep in his heart, who found it difficult to truly appreciate anything that life offered. But slowly with each passing day, with each tender hug shared and smile offered, my bitterness dissolved, my sadness dissipated and my aching soul began to heal. Every time my arms opened to the world around me, my heart opened as well.

But I did find that making each hug as authentic and spontaneous as the next was not always easy, especially when I was hugging hundreds of people consecutively. It was important to me that each and every person I hugged received my equal attention and affection. In order to remain grounded and connected to my heart, I decided that after each hug I would place my palms on my heart centre and take a brief moment to express gratitude. Then, guided by my breath, I would open my arms out to the world once again. It was through this ritual gesture that the five principles of hugging were born: hugging with respect, hugging without condition, hugging with gratitude, hugging with heart and hugging the moment. (I've laid these principles out in detail in part 3 of the book.)

The Kaleidoscope of Humanity

I was at the square seven days a week, ten hours a day, for months on end; only day-long downpours kept me home. It was a gruelling schedule, but I loved it. Hugging people enlivened me in a way that I had never experienced before. I was so excited every morning to get back to my corner on the square to hug and hug some more that it didn't matter if my body was tired. I wanted to live this great adventure completely, and not miss a moment of it. I felt that profound changes were taking place within my mind and heart. I was happier, more serene, and wiser with each passing day. I was becoming whole. I was in love with the beauty of hugging life and I couldn't get enough of it. My intention had evolved from one of bringing pleasure to others with the expectation of money to bringing loving kindness for nothing more than the joy of doing so. As the intention that guided my hugs became more selfless and loving, more love and abundance filled my life. Hugging with heart had become manna for my soul. It was my joy, my raison d'être! So, fatigued or not, off I went, under clouds or sunshine, to take in one more day of my amazing experience.

All of that being said, my journey as public hugger has not been without its struggles and challenges. In spite of the popularity of the Hugger Busker, I was constantly dealing with cynical, aggressive and malevolent energies. The harsh reality of performing in the street was challenging for me at times; it was hard on my ego and my confidence. Though I am streetwise, I also have a certain naïve innocence about me that allows me to view the world through rose-coloured glasses. Though this peachy view is one of my great strengths, it's also the source of my endless struggle with accepting the Divine ugliness of human existence as well as its exquisite beauty.

There were days when nobody cared about getting hugged and I was simply ignored; this disappointed me. There were times when I had to fend off vicious drunks who would ambush me when I least expected it; this frightened me. There were moments when I had to face the curses of embittered fellow artists who, feeling threatened by my popularity, would spend their days figuring out ways to intimidate me and my audience; this hurt me. I had to remain constantly vigilant of youthful skaters who would whiz by and try to steal my money; this angered me. I encountered rude and obnoxious types who would blow smoke in my face, throw food at me or grossly grope me and then insult me for resisting; these people would try my patience, and bring out the worst in me.

There before me streamed the kaleidoscope of humanity, and I was willing to hug them all. But in spite of my openness of heart and my loving intentions, there were days when I just couldn't handle it. I would blow my fuse and start cursing. On occasion I even chased an offender out of the square. Not very loving, I know. But at the time it was the only way I knew how to respond. It seemed that my generosity of spirit, the goodness that I was offering, was too much for some people to deal with and so they had to tarnish or damage it somehow. I wanted to believe that goodness would bring harmony and peace to my world, yet when discordance and malevolence came calling I was plunged into inner turmoil once again. I found it increasingly difficult to accept the reactions that such situations stirred up in me. My inability to cope harmoniously with the discordant elements of life caused me much sadness and frustration, and I all too often found myself responding to conflict with conflict. In a way I was still throwing my bike at cars.

Without the kindness of strangers who believed in what I was doing and the ongoing support of my family, I would not have made it through the summer. My mom, my dad, Annik and Jade came by regularly to watch me. They would bring me a sandwich, a slice of watermelon, a chilled chai latte, or just their loving affection. Their supportive presence brought me the strength and courage I needed to persevere through the toughest days. It made me realize how beautiful and empowering it was to be loved. To them I am eternally grateful, and I cherish their constant presence in my life.

The Student of Life

I regret those times that I became angry, aggressive or abusive towards others, but I also realize now that these situations were important lessons for me to learn. Standing out there, day in and day out, at the mercy of human nature, was very hard on my ego, which was constantly taking a beating. But on the other hand it was exactly that experience that helped me move forward. It was through the malevolent actions of others that I came to see my own ugliness, and that allowed me to face it, resolve it and move beyond it into a new paradigm of thought and behaviour. How could I not then love these people? They were my teachers, my guides, come into my life to help me face my own struggles and inadequacies so that I could evolve as an individual. I was a good student; I learned my lessons well, as each incident came to a better conclusion then the preceding one. It took me a full year before I was able to embrace the dark and light side of human nature with equanimity, serenity, appreciation and compassionate caring.

There was, however, as "Dr. Phil" McGraw likes to say, a "defining moment" in my personal evolution that helped me find the beginnings of inner peace and thus make way for unconditional love to fully bloom. I remember the day well. It was a warm, sunny day at noon; the air was fragrant and breezy, and many office and city workers were hurrying about to get their lunch or were already sitting on benches eating it. It was one of those times when I was being ignored by the masses. This bothered me not at all; I was happily floating in silence and mindful awareness of all that surrounded me. The sounds, the smells, my breath, the sensations within me and around me all melted together so that I could no longer differentiate between then. My being became all that surrounded me and in turn my surroundings became me.

I stood on my little Persian rug, observing the flow of people around me without judgment. As if my tinted glasses had been lifted from my eyes, my vision cleared and I began to recognize myself in each and every person that walked by. I could see my sad self, my fearful self, my angry self, my hurt self, my cheerful self, my preoccupied self, my egotistical self, my macho self, my exuberant self, my distracted self, my anxious self, my playful self. On and on, reflections of my selves passed by me. I was all these people and they were all me! The exterior packaging was different, but the rest was identical. It was astonishing to witness my selves being themselves!

In that moment it became very clear to me that the first step to loving myself was to accept who I was totally, unconditionally and without judgment, and that the first step to loving others unconditionally was to accept them exactly as they were, not as I wanted them to be. This didn't mean that I had to like or agree with another person's behaviour or life choices, but rather that I must be compassionate towards their human nature, their human suffering, and their human struggle, because they were also my nature, my suffering, and my struggle.

It was as if a huge load had been lifted from my shoulders, and I began to laugh out loud. People looked at me quite strangely but I didn't care; I had found a touch of paradise and that was worth celebrating! The breeze shifted with my joyful outburst, and I was no longer ignored. I hugged non-stop for the rest of the day. From that day on, I began trying to approach people who struggled with physical or emotional intimacy with gentleness and understanding, rather than criticism and judgment as I had in the past. I was grateful to God for opening my mind and heart to this profound insight and I hoped that I would have the wisdom to honour the gift of inner peace.

Hugging Downtown

Fall was quickly approaching, so I decided that it was time to take my hugs to the corporate suits and skirts of downtown. I figured that if any one group of people needed hugs, it was the denizens of officedom. I arrived early on a crisp but sunny day and found a perfect spot near the entrance of a classy shopping complex. I had barely finished setting up when two mall security guards arrived and aggressively ordered me to move five feet beyond some invisible line on the sidewalk as I was apparently too close to their building. Who's to argue with testosterone in uniform? So I moved.

They must have been a bad omen, because it just went downhill from there. As the trickle of pedestrians slowly grew, so did the stream of beggars, peddlers, preachers and artisans. By noon I found myself one of many who lined the downtown sidewalks plying their wares and their cares. There was everything from "Your name on a grain of rice!" to bottle cap jewellery, from painted photographs to African carvings, from "God will save you if you repent!" to hot rollerblade babes hawking toothpaste, from gaggles of pitiful beggars and legless veterans to me with my cheerful smile and heartfelt hugs. There we were, all of us on the same sidewalk side by side, vying for the attention of people who were hurried, harried and hungry to fill an insatiable inner void with material pleasures. We were simply an unwelcome obstruction in their quest to placate their dissatisfaction. I realized that with all the store windows, billboards and street hawkers, there was so much going on to attract people's attention and wallets that to many I just became another guy trying to con them out of a dollar with a sentimental concept.

Then I noticed a past Prime Minister and one of Canada's biggest financiers chatting just a few feet from me. So I did what any bold hugger would do: I plucked up my charm and offered them a hug. I got a disdainful glance and cold silence instead as they moved away. Their reaction didn't surprise me in the least; in fact I would have been surprised had they accepted. But the attempt was worth the contempt.

Over the next few weeks I tried several times to give hugs downtown, but each was as unsatisfying as the next, for both the public and me. Not that there weren't any takers, but there were just a handful out of thousands. It just was not worth the energy. I had to find a more suitable environment or way to get people to hug. What saddened me most about was that most of the people who passed me by looked so unhappy and weary, with grim faces, downcast eyes and shoulders folded inward. I just wanted to shout at them, to shake them, to wake them up so they would just stop for a moment and really see the beauty of the day. I wanted them to really see what it was I was offering them. I so badly wanted to hug all these unhappy people who just refused to acknowledge their need for tender loving, let alone give in to it. One day, a person said to me, "If I hug you I might just break down and weep, and I can't allow myself to do that." What a sad state our world is in. So I went back to the square for the rest of the fall season.

Though my experiences downtown were not fruitful, they helped me realize the importance of my quest. Downtown is a harsh yet seductive master to many urbanites, driving them to become slaves to their egocentric habits, to their worries, to their harried lifestyles. Maybe they weren't inspired by the Hugger Busker, but I was certainly inspired by them—enough to write this book. I figured that if I was not able to touch them with my hugs, then maybe I could move them with my words.

"It is alarming how sceptical we are of good intentions. We think nothing is for free, and if someone tries to give you something for free, be ready for the catch, don't believe it.

A well-dressed man stands, arms outstretched, in front of a sign reading 'Free Hugs.' Business is slow. Most people walk right by. Some stop to read the sign, but they smile, shake their heads 'No!' and walk on. But there are some few who believe.

Some will stop and hug the stranger, because they can see clearly this man has devoted himself to the cause of spreading joy by offering tokens of compassion.

Bless this man. He knows something the crowds walking by do not.

Active love is generated by the conscious decision to have a positive impact. A hug is a physical gesture of love, an embrace of acceptance, a primal connection.

We share our human condition. We share this world. These things we have in common.

The sceptics need to open their eyes to the truth, their hearts to brotherly love, and their arms to the hug of a kind gentleman.

Truly, this is an act of beauty."
- Joel C., Quebec, Canada

The above is one of several poems left in the Hugger Busker's donation tin. There are many sceptics in the world but hopefully my actions will convince some of them that strangers are just friends, lovers, or teachers waiting to be discovered.

Make a Wish

By the end of the summer I had been noticing the emergence of an interesting phenomenon. Whenever I thought of a need—for something to drink, for a fresh lapel flower, for some food, for some friendly encouragement—what I needed would appear. Within hours of my wishing for it, the things I wished for would manifest. I was quite astounded by the growing frequency and regularity of this occurrence. People would just walk up to me and offer me refreshment, or a flower, or some food, or a kind word.

About this same time, I started thinking how wonderful it would be to make a small documentary about the Hugger Busker and all the fascinating people who came for hugs. Miraculously, the same phenomenon happened with the documentary. One day I was feeling very sad because the summer was coming to an end and I hadn't documented any of my beautiful experiences. I thought "If only I knew someone who could do this for me, it would make me so happy." The very next afternoon my friend Charlie dropped by with her new beau, who just happened to be a film producer. He loved what I was doing and by the following weekend he and a small crew were shooting footage of the Hugger Busker in action.

From the moment I became aware of the connection between my desire and the manifestation of that desire, that occurrence has been taking place more and more often. Even though I don't quite understand it, I continue to be amazed by it. I have figured out that when my inner intention is selfless and loving and I hold no expectations, then whatever I desire will manifest itself. On the other hand, if my desire is ego-gratifying and I'm attached to a specific outcome, then it won't happen. So now, when I most need something, I simply turn to my heart and ask God within to guide me, and everything I need comes to me in one form or another. I don't worry anymore whether a plan will work out or not, because I know in my heart that when I surrender to the Divine flow of life, things unfold exactly as they should.

The documentary shoot went smoothly; every detail fell into place, and all kinds of delightful and touching people and situations appeared as the camera was rolling. It seemed that the best and most interesting examples of what I had been experiencing all summer came to life in those few days we filmed. The material was extraordinary! Unfortunately, the final footage was not of broadcast quality, so I couldn't make a marketable documentary out of it. Still, I had enough suitable footage to make a decent promotional demo for the Hugger Busker, a project I worked on during the first part of winter.

Creating the demo gave me the motivation to try and get proper funding to make a feature-length documentary about hugging and public huggers around the world. So I set out to write a professional documentary feature film proposal. I shopped it around to several producers and film houses but it seems that conflict and drama is more marketable these days than love and hugs. I was surprised to realize that while I felt a bit disappointed at the refusals, they didn't deter me or upset me; in a sense it was as though I had been expecting them. I know for certain that this documentary will be made the way I envision it when the time is ripe, and when the people involved have followed their heart to my doorstep, just like all those who have help make this book a reality.

The upside is that all the months I spent researching and writing the proposal brought me to writing this book. For me, it seems that a positive path always emerges from every seemingly negative one, if I just trust that every moment is a stepping stone to my fulfillment, whether I know what will fulfill me or not. One step back or one step forward—each has its rightful place in my evolution, so I try to embrace them with equal enthusiasm.

By the time spring arrived I was in great spirits. I was very excited that April and May had given me some warm, sunny weekends so that I could start giving hugs again. I had missed hugging terribly during the winter, sitting alone in front of my computer writing and editing. The few indoor events that the Hugger Busker was invited to felt like just a teaser to keep me hungry and excited about the coming summer. The winter break was good for me as it gave me time to reflect on and assimilate what I had experienced the year before. The process of inner transformation needs time to settle in the psyche before it can manifest as discernible change. Like a good wine, experience must sit undisturbed for a time before it can reach its full potential. The winter finally ended, the snow disappeared, the trees began to bud, the flowers to bloom and I was primed for a new season of hugging.

Princesses, Angels and Paupers

My second year was a series of strange, wild, frightful, wonderful, difficult and powerful adventures. Every day brought me a vast array of people and situations to stimulate and challenge my mind, heart and spirit. I was a very different man than the previous year; joyfulness, lightness of being, a warm easy smile and a cheerful demeanour had become integral parts of how I now expressed myself. I was happy and carefree, and it showed in my attitude, but more importantly in my hugs. My gratitude and appreciation for the life I was leading came through in all my actions. People reacted differently as well; more were inclined to share a hug with me and, much to their surprise, many stayed in my arms longer than they expected they normally would have with a stranger.

The year began in a most noble way. Gerald Tremblay, the mayor of Montreal, stopped by with Her Royal Highness Princess Margriet of the Netherlands. I bowed humbly and welcomed her to our beautiful city. Aware that hugging royalty was not proper protocol, I offered to kiss her hand. She graciously accepted. With reverence and tenderness I kissed the royal hand and she in turn laughed with delight. I wished her a happy day and I returned to my stillness as they wandered off smiling. It was very thrilling for me to have kissed the hand of a real princess. It's every little boy's dream, and I am a little boy at heart! It was a fabulous way to begin a season of hugging—not with a hug, but with one more dream fulfilled.

When I asked Jade how she viewed my personal evolution over the past two years, she described it in this way: "Your first year," she said, "was one of personal transformation, and your second was one of spiritual transmutation." As my approach to life evolved, so did my hugs, taking on a much more spiritual and healing quality. During my frequent periods of stillness I began practicing metta, or loving kindness meditation, and Reiki, the circulation of healing energy. As the days progressed so did the strength and potency of the energy that flowed through me. I could feel it vibrating from the ground into my feet and up through my heart, head and hands. As with hugging, I did not consciously set out to explore these disciplines; I just found myself naturally drawn to them. Hugging someone became a whole new experience for me, and for the people I hugged as well. The act of hugging was now less about performance and more about my deep desire to share the nurturing power of love with as many people as possible. As I touched the hearts of strangers, so strangers came to touch my heart.

A woman approached me one morning and after hugging me told me that she was a chaperone for the Amadeus Chorale. She asked if I would mind if her girls sang for me, as they wanted to show appreciation for my heartfelt art by sharing their artistry with me. How could I refuse such an offer? As I stood in stillness, with my arms outstretched, I sensed a group of people place themselves behind me. I was graced with the most sublime and uplifting version of Alleluia that I had ever heard. Angelic voices filled the square. These were angels sent to fill my being with love and grace and to remind me that I too am worthy of the unconditional love of strangers. Knowing that these young singers were giving their breath and their heart to bring me joy touched me so deeply that tears began to stream down my face. I was experiencing one of those all-too-rare moments in life when the exquisite beauty of God reveals itself in all its glory. When they finished singing I slowly turned to thank them. There before me stood twenty or so teenage angels, all with the most beautiful smiles. I had become so overtaken with emotion that I could barely get a word out, so I simply placed my hands over my heart and bowed to them with reverence and humility. I was filled with such gratitude to them and to God for having brought me this deeply moving moment. It made me realize that each hug can become an act of gratitude and reverence for the spirit of life. This event had such a profound impact on me that I am still moved to tears as I sit here writing about it.

I endeavour to never discriminate in whom I hug; irrespective of social class, economic standing, age, physical or mental ability, race, or creed, everyone is welcome in my circle of love. Being human is the only criteria, though I do make exceptions for friendly pets and alien beings. There are a number of hostels and soup kitchens for the homeless in the area around the square and many of these poor but generous souls pass me daily. Many of them look unkempt, unwashed and diseased, but we need to look past their appearances and remember they are worthy of our respect and kindness. Quite a few come for hugs, others stop by to chat, and some come for energy healing. The year before, Jade, who is a Reiki Master, initiated me into the practice of Reiki, and I became a certified practitioner. In the original spirit of this healing art I do not charge for a healing and I only offer it to those who are most in need, the homeless, for that is how Reiki began—as a healing practice offered to the poor and destitute in the slums of Tokyo.

When I take a shabbily dressed homeless man into my arms and give him a hug right after sharing an equally tender one with an elegant couple, the disconcerted looks of surprise on the faces of passers-by is very amusing. But I know that the homeless appreciate my respectful attitude. They maybe down and out, but that doesn't make them less worthy of love and respect. It saddens me that they are continuously pushed aside and put down with words and glances. A few have even dropped change in my donation tin, or placed fruit next to it. I know that they are sharing their tiny fortune with me. At first I tried to dissuade this but they seemed so happy to do it, and eventually I realized that it would be disrespectful if I didn't accept their generosity.

These beautiful souls were teaching me to live and to hug with respect for all beings. Their gestures were born of true generosity. Sure, I love receiving hundred-dollar bills from wealthy people, but receiving an apple from a homeless man is priceless. Many of us see so many beggars in our downtown streets that we just ignore them. I don't ignore them anymore. If I can't offer change then I offer a kind greeting, letting them know that even though I am not donating to their cause I am still acknowledging their presence. Recognizing someone's existence can be worth so much more then a quarter thrown dismissively in their cup.

Blissful Inspiration

The Old Port is at the bottom of the hill from the square where I stand. I decided to buy a permit to perform there as well. It was an expensive decision but it turned out to be a very wise one. This is where I attracted the largest crowds, shared the most healing hugs and experienced the events that sealed my spiritual transmutation.

On Wednesday and Saturday evenings during the months of June and July, Montreal hosts an international fireworks competition, held at the water's edge. Every summer, tens of thousands of people gather in the Old Port to watch and marvel at the fiery spectacle. I had been given a choice location right at the entrance of the Port under a huge spotlight, where hundreds could watch me hug.

There I stood facing my Lady of the Sea, as I affectionately called the Madonna that stands perched on the dome of the church by the Old Port, who stands with arms open wide inviting all those in need of comfort into her bosom. I don't know if it was because I was closer to the water, or because I was facing east, or because two months of loving kindness (metta) meditation had raised my level of energy, but those nights my ability to fill others with loving vibrations and to reach blissful states of rapture was overwhelming. As the tenderness in my heart grew I began to find a rhythm of hugging and stillness, of silence and bliss.

I shared hundreds upon hundreds of deeply loving hugs on those evenings. During some hugs it seemed as if time had literally stopped, and we both became lost in the glorious oneness of the embrace. Each hug became a beautiful and fulfilling experience irrespective of how long it lasted or the form it took. I was finally letting go of ego, judgment and expectation. I was hugging the moment and life was hugging back. In some instances the person or people that I took into my arms became part of me and we merged into a single entity of breath and vibration. It was an extraordinary sensation to actually feel the vibrations of loving energy flow from my heart through another person's body and out into my hand as it rested on their back. I could have held those hugs for an eternity. The comfort, the warmth, the communion of human spirit, and the all-encompassing sensation of shared oneness became as exquisite as anything I had ever experienced. It was all so new to me. I wasn't certain what to do so I did nothing; I just continued hugging. Just as having a chorus of angels singing Alleluia was utterly sublime, these luminous hugs were utterly Divine.

I knew they affected me deeply, but how much effect could a simple, heartfelt hug really have on someone? I often wonder what happens to people after I share a hug with them. Did this moment of human tenderness affect them somehow? Was their mood altered? Was their day transformed for the better? Was their perception of life changed in any significant way? The only inkling I ever had was when people wrote their comments in my guestbook. From these touching testimonials I learned that my loving actions did indeed give many people pause for reflection, and actually allowed some to re-evaluate their fears of human intimacy and their desire to share loving kindness with others. But what made me truly see the life-affirming power of hugging was an e-mail I received from a young woman:

"Just wanted to let you know what a difference you made in my life. These last few months have been mostly a living hell for me. One evening walking in the Old Port I saw this kind of funny-looking guy offering hugs. Usually I hate being touched, by any means, but I went for one of those hugs... You changed my whole life. From that day I decided that suicide wasn't the solution. So now every morning I look at a picture of me in your arms and I know that I can go along with life. It may be stupid, but thank you for saving my life."
- Pamela F., Quebec, Canada

This young woman's words have reverberated deeply in my heart. When I began this journey it never occurred to me that a simple act of kindness such as a hug, a smile, a supportive word or loving gesture would brighten my life to the degree it has, nor did I imagine the effect it would have on the lives of others. If our words and actions can carry such healing power, then I invite you to take a moment every day to smile warmly to a stranger. You might just be offering them the spark of hope they need to face the rest of their day with renewed life.

It became very clear that my performance had taken on a whole new dimension. In fact it was no longer performance, but a calling, as I had become a channel or a conduit for the healing energy of universal love. Couples, individuals, small groups of strangers, and whole families came to me on those glorious evenings and some spent four or five minutes in my arms absorbing the energy that emanated from me. It was an incredible experience for me to see the delighted and amazed expressions on people's faces as they walked away from the embrace. Some trembled and were giddy with emotion, and others laughed; some were in tears, while others drifted away enveloped in a profound silence.

Hugging Violence

During one of my own silent moments, as I looked out towards the setting sun, a great calm came over me like a soothing wave that washed away all tension, worry and fear. In that instant the world around me broke into pieces and reassembled itself anew. There was no longer a separation between myself and what was outside of me. As the previous year I had recognized myself in all others, I now found myself in all that is. It was what I had experienced as a child when I had become one with the essence of God. I was swept away in rapturous bliss. You could have taken all my money, my cases, and every stitch of clothing on my body that moment, and it would not have mattered because I was alive. I had awakened to the truth of my very being, as a being of God.

Just then, my bliss was shattered. A man approached me for a hug, and when I came to wrap my arms around him, he aggressively hit me in the chest with his hands, pushing me into the lamppost behind me. I had been in such an open and vulnerable state that I trembled with the shock of it. I kept asking him why he had done this, and as he backed away he mocked me—he just kept mirroring my gestures and repeating what I was saying. He then joined his friends and left. At least three hundred people watched this and only a few reacted and booed him. But I just stood there, mouth agape, a stunned expression on my face. I was terribly shaken. Thankfully several people came to offer me support by holding me in their arms. People asked me to continue giving hugs, and told me I shouldn't let someone like that destroy the good that I was doing. It took all my energy but I began hugging again and slowly I regained my rhythm. Still, my energetic connection was broken and I could not recuperate it that evening.

For the next month, this kind of experience became a cycle. I would go to the Old Port for the fireworks, hug hundreds of people, reach ecstatic bliss, and then at the height of it I would get physically attacked.

It wasn't as bad as it sounds. In fact, every time I was confronted, I was able to react with less devastation and more equanimity. I was beginning to understand that there is always a balance in the universe, and positive energy attracts negative energy. Hostile individuals were drawn to me in order to transform my energy to theirs. The less I gave in to their vibrations by reacting in fear or aggression, the less power they had over me. To counter my fear I had to completely surrender to the power of love and see even my attackers with compassionate eyes. It was a mighty challenge. For most of my life, violence and aggression raised such fear and turmoil in me that I had always responded with equal aggression and anger.

The last attack was by far the most dangerous and volatile. A highly intoxicated, drugged man— who, as I found out later, had not taken his anti-psychosis medication—was intimidating everyone around the square so they would give him money. He wasn't getting any, so he decided that I was going to give him some, but first he wanted to intimidate me.

This small, scared, red-eyed man stood a foot in front of me, his muscles tensed, his fist cocked and ready to put through my face. I just looked at him with a smile and breathed deeply and with as much serenity as I could muster I offered him a hug rather than money. We stood there toe to toe. Time slowed down, my heart raced, and every fibre of my being wanted to strike before he did, but calm seemed to take hold of me. I knew that I was not facing the man himself but rather the alcohol and drugs that had enslaved him. How could I not look at this sad, miserable man with compassion? It would do no good for me to hurt him, so I just continued to look at him with a gentle smile.

He was not too pleased that I didn't respond to his threats. But since I gave him nothing to bounce his rage off, he left to find other victims until the police arrived to cart him away screaming and cussing.

I had remained calm on the outside, but I was shaking like a leaf inside. For the first time in my life I had diffused a violent situation with calm and dignity. I was very proud of myself, as I knew that my journey had taken me far. A year before, I had been the one running around screaming and cussing, but on that day I had found the courage to face my fears and instead show loving kindness to someone truly in need of it. This is when the true meaning of hugging without condition took root in me.

A Hugger's Life

I feel blessed to have been offered such deeply moving and life-changing experiences. I believe more then ever that one reaps what one sows, and I am happy that sowing love in the world has become my passion and joy.

I am honoured by the many gifts and tokens of appreciation that people continue to bring me—money, flowers, candy, refreshments, poems, drawings, healing talismans and good-luck charms. I am humbled and a little overwhelmed by the number of people who have asked me to pray for them or on them. I truly hope that their prayers are answered and that their suffering is healed. For those that have bowed before me in respectful reverence, I hope that your gesture be directed towards the essence of God that lays within each of us and not towards me, the man. I may have gifts, but I'm like everyone else—rife with insecurities, weaknesses, cravings and pettiness. The most I can do is offer prayers, loving kindness and heartfelt hugs to whoever needs them. For the rest I place myself in God's loving hands.

Where this great journey is to lead me, I have yet to discover. But I am certain that no matter where I end up, getting there will have been an incredibly rewarding experience. My quest to change my world one hug at a time is slowly gaining support—locally, nationally and even internationally. Amazing opportunities have presented themselves to me since I began and they continue to do so in the most auspicious and unexpected manner, just as adventures should. As each day passes, the Hugger Busker welcomes into his embrace countless fascinating and wonderful people, all part of his delightfully strange and beautiful story. Sharing my journey with you, through the process of writing this book, has made me realize that there are still so many more stories to recount and inspiring moments to share that "A Hugger's Life" may merit more then just a chapter... it might very well deserve a book of its own.

As I continue hugging in the street, at charitable and promotional events, and at festivals and fairs around the world, the adventures continue and so does my evolution. Through my performance, my writing, my documentary and my speaking engagements I hope to continue to inspire others to approach their life with loving kindness so that they, too, can find fulfillment and happiness by hugging life and each other.

"I saw you and only later did it hit me that while we should all try to do at least one kind gesture each day, here you were doing dozens of them every day. After I returned to Florida I went right out, spoke to my neighbours, hugged them and said I was so happy we lived next door to each other."
 - Allen O., Florida, USA

- 2 -

ABOUT HUGGING

My journey as a hugger has inspired many reflections, some of which I offer to you here as a series of short essays. Enjoy them in whatever order you please!

The Roots of Hugging

From the beginning of time, the hug has been an integral part of humans' instinctive tools for survival, whether it's used as a sign of affection or kinship, as a fighting technique, or simply as a way to keep warm against the elements. Hugging finds its roots in the comfort and safety of our mothers' first embrace. When we first come into being we are primarily tactile creatures, exploring and identifying our world mostly through touch. As our mind develops we begin experiencing life on different levels, and our need to touch lessens. Then, as behavioural codes set in and language becomes the primary tool for communication, our natural desire to touch others diminishes and may even become completely repressed. Even so, our primal need to hold, touch or cling to one another never entirely disappears. Touch is an instinctive response for most humans seeking comfort and safety.

Hugging has developed over time to express a wide variety of emotions, psychological states and relationship dynamics. Each hug is unique, and can reflect a multitude of nuances and meanings depending on the individuals involved, the situation and the message or feeling that the giver wishes to convey. Hugs can be used to show tenderness, affection, concern, nurturing, consolation, reconciliation, compassion, love, passion, desire, friendship, kinship, support, desperation, grief, dependence, possessiveness, control, dominance and aggression... just for starters!

There remains one constant: the hug, no matter what form it takes, is the single most powerful physical act we use to express our innate need for human warmth, bonding and acceptance. Whether we do it with strangers or intimates, this simple gesture, when shared in a truly heartfelt and loving way, has the power to uplift, transform, and heal people. Touch is as fundamental to the sustenance of human beings as air, water, nourishment and shelter. If our lives are devoid of human tenderness, then our bodies will sicken, our hearts will harden and our spirit will wither. After all, we are intrinsically social animals. We may be shy, introverted, reserved or even sociophobic, but we still need to be in the presence of and interact with other human beings if we are to thrive.

The Healing Power of Hugging

Over the years, many clinical and psychological studies have looked at the therapeutic effects of human touch. Studies undertaken by the Touch Research Institutes at the University of Miami School of Medicine reveal that there is an important correlation between human touch and individuals' psychological, emotional and physical well-being. Research elsewhere has also shown that massage and therapeutic touch help reduce stress, aggression, anxiety and depression; they heighten awareness and boost the immune system.

My own conclusion, based on my personal experiences of hugging and speaking with thousands of people, is that hugging brings these benefits not just to the receiver but to the giver as well.

With the rapid advancement of technology over the past decade, communication, entertainment, merchandise, sex, friendship and even love can find their way into our homes and lives without our ever having to step outside the door. Technology has effectively made it that much easier for people to live in physical isolation while maintaining contact with the outside world.

This growing trend towards social isolationism is making us lose touch with ourselves as loving beings and what being human in a human society can be. People from all walks of life have become disillusioned, disenfranchised and disconnected. So it is not surprising that many of the therapies and healing techniques that have emerged in the past few decades focus on touch, hugging, laughter, and physical expression as tools to help patients reconnect with their creative, feeling selves. If we only expressed our love and caring more freely to ourselves and to one another, we might not need such therapies to heal. Hugging is not the answer to all our ills, but when used in a loving and unconditional way it is a potent, unlimited source of natural life-giving and healing energy.

What kind of hugger are you?

ACADEMIC — You'll observe hugging, study its effects, even lecture on its benefits, but when it comes down to it you never actually hug anyone.

ALPHA – There is purpose and drive in your hugs; they are all power and business.

AGGRESSIVE – Like a wrestling linebacker, you force your opponent to submit to your back-pounding dominance.

ANGRY – Yes, there are angry huggers out there, who love hating to love.

BASHFUL – You become coy and blush all over before every hug.

CASUAL – Uncommitted but friendly, with maybe a pat on the back for posterity.

COMPULSIVE – If you can't find a tree to hug, any mailbox will do.

COOL – You bring style and flair to your hugging moves.

CUDDLY – With PJs and teddy bear at the ready, you are always ready for a cuddling party.

CURSORY – You hug because you have to, so let's get it over with.

CYBER – ({) [ ] []:** (()) (((((hug me))))) >:D< (})

DELICATE – You just wouldn't want to wrinkle your outfit or get a bruise.

DISCORDANT – There is no rhythm or rhyme to your brand of loving.

DYNAMIC – All power and emotion, there is no getting out of your hugs.

EMOTIONAL – You just break down in tears at the first squeeze of an embrace.

FASHIONABLE – Graceful and sleek, you sashay into a hug and leave it unruffled.

FORMAL – Cool and calculated for maximum effect with the minimum of commitment.

GIGGLER – You can't help but giggle uncontrollably whenever someone hugs you.

HABITUAL – Like clockwork, you hug at the same place, same time, the same people.

HEALING – Your energy flow heals everything and everyone you touch.

INTIMATE – You hug only when in love.

IN DENIAL – You adamantly deny needing or even wanting a hug until you get one, and then you cry your eyes out.

JEALOUS – You have a fit if you partner hugs anyone other than you, even when it's their mother.

KINKY – A hug is only fun when one of you is bound and blindfolded.

LANGUOROUS – Your hugs last and last and… well, it might as well be a cuddle because you're not letting go!

MASTER – You've hugged so many people that your
hugging technique is a veritable art form.

MULTI-PERSON – The more the merrier, the bigger the
better!

MULTI-TASKER – You hug, talk on the phone, eat, drive
and try to do it all NOW!

NEEDY – When someone has you in their embrace you
just don't want to let go. Ever.

NEUROTIC – Hugging can be therapy, just don't take it
out on us.

NURTURING – You coddle and cradle and mother your
way into people's hearts.

ORNERY – You grumble and complain about how
you never get hugs, but only while getting
hugged.

PATIENT – You wait and wait and wait for the right
moment… and then they hug someone else.

QUESTIONING – You want to hug me?! Why? Are you
sure? You're not sick, are you?

ROMANTIC – Everyone who hugs you might just be your
soulmate!

RUSHED – Hey, love you, but let me go, because I really
got to go, to where I don't know.

Selfless — You hate hugging; you only do it because it brings joy to other people's lives.

Sensual — Only with the candles lit and the clothes off.

Sexual — Just the thought of it gets you aroused.

Submissive — You love pleasing others so much that you'll gladly submit to any hugging request.

Telekinetic — All you have to do is think about getting hugged and someone will hug you.

Uncommitted — You always seem to find yourself in the arms of people you care little for.

Variant — You've hugged so often that you now invent your own hugs to keep things fresh.

Wishy-Washy — You want one, but you don't, but then you do, but just a little one.

Xtasy — Oh, dude! This hug is sooo like WOW! Yeah, incredibly cool! I want to hug you forever!

Yogi — Your hugs are wholesome, strong, spiritual and grounded, but you have to be aligned and balanced first.

Zealous — Your passion for hugging is such that you've even written a book about it.

Who Is a Hugger?

Every single person on this planet is a potential hugger.

In my first months of my hugging career I made it a game to try and guess who would hug me and who would not. I quickly discovered that this was an impossible proposition. There was no identifying a hugger by character, dress or demeanour. For example, when I was certain that the bohemian couple sauntering by would indulge they would ignore me, just as a group of football jocks would throw themselves into my waiting embrace wholeheartedly. When I thought that the jet-set diva dressed for the opera and her Armani-clad escort would turn their nose up at me, I would find myself wrapped in their embrace sharing a most intimate hug, while the youth prayer group who I believed would delight in my offer of unconditional love preferred proselytizing to hugging.

I've long since stopped trying to figure out who would hug me. Instead I decided to view everyone who crosses my path as a potential hugger—which they are, even if they don't yet know it.

The Gender of Hugging

I am often asked if I hug more women or men, with the assumption being that the answer will be "women." But that is not the case. Neither gender hugs more or less than the other.

Let me speak of tendencies rather then certainties. I find that women bring more tenderness, emotion and vulnerability to their hugs. Women tend to be more comfortable hugging other women, and those in their intimate circle. They will shy away from hugging men they don't know well unless they feel confident that there are no sexual implications. They will allow themselves to receive and give affection freely when they feel safe, though they are careful not to let their touch be misinterpreted as anything other then friendly. Women complain that men do not show enough tenderness when hugging, and that they will often linger, sending mixed signals as if they expect more intimacy when none is desired.

Men bring physical strength and a spirit of camaraderie to their hugs. They tend to be less expressive emotionally, less touchy-feely, and they seem more comfortable hugging family, close friends or team-mates. They are more hesitant to hug a man in public than they are to hug a woman, but when they do hug me it will either be a strong, physical hug or just a quick, friendly pat on the back. They are less inclined to show actual tender affection. Fathers who once enjoyed hugging and cuddling their young daughters tend to become less comfortable being physically demonstrative with them when the girls start looking more like young women. Sons will usually imitate their fathers' behaviour when it comes to the how they express affection physically with other men and women. I have witnessed many fathers aggressively insist that their son get a hug from me, yet they will adamantly refuse to hug me themselves. It is no great surprise that the boy then also adamantly refuses to be hugged.

Though these generalities represent the traits I have commonly seen among men and women, no approach is exclusive to a specific gender, nor are they reflective of an individual's hugging potential. Who hugs and how they hug has less to do with gender and more to do with an individual's ability or willingness to share physical intimacy. Shyness, insecurity, fear of being judged, discomfort with being held or touched—these things have nothing to do with gender but rather with conditions of personal upbringing and character traits.

Children

I love hugging children. They bring such heartfelt sincerity to their displays of affection that it is utterly inspiring. We have so much to learn from them and so much to remember. Their exuberance for life and their inexhaustible curiosity remind me to banish my adult pretences and approach my world anew, with wonderment, spontaneous delight, and unconditional love. This is what children teach me to remember.

A group of fifty tiny tots, out on an excursion, sat down in front of me one morning to watch my stillness. As I always do in such cases, I waited for them to settle down and then I looked into their bright, curious eyes. Moving with deliberate slowness, so as not to scare them, I greeted them. Some were startled, others were mesmerized, but it is when I offered to hug them that their excitement became evident. At first there was a moment of suspended silence, but as they grasped what was being offered the giggles and the chatter began. One after the other they came, from the boldest to the shyest, opening their small arms to receive my tender embrace as they offered an equally loving one in return. Some even came for seconds and thirds, while others left a penny or two in my donation tin. It was touching to see a child dig into their pocket for a coin to offer me. Their gratitude was apparent, and I in turn was grateful to receive their spontaneous and genuine expressions of loving tenderness. I offered hugs to the chaperones as well; with some hesitancy, as if hugging was just a "child's thing," they accepted, eliciting happy shrieks from the children.

It is easy to philosophize, complain, or give advice; as we are usually not forced to live up to our words even when we expect others to adhere to our perceptions of life. How many of us walk the talk? Daily I hear parents, especially fathers, admonish their sons for refusing to hug me, yet when I offer the same parent a hug they will refuse and back away just like their child did moments before them. What a fine example they set. This "do as I say, not as I do" attitude is terribly hypocritical, and believe me, children notice and remember. Too often, I see parents give their kids a quick, cursory hug or pat on the back when it is clear that the child is asking for real affection rather then just attention. It saddens me. These parents don't seem to realize that they are the primary role models for their children and that their child will end up emulating many of their behaviours and attitudes.

It is obvious to me that physically affectionate parents tend to instil a desire and an appreciation for physical affection in their children, just as reticent or physically distant parents instil the same fearful attitudes in their offspring. When a child asks for a hug, why not give them one? And make it a real one! This way they learn that they are worthy of being loved and that physical affection can be positive and welcome. In return their delicious gift of pure love will touch your heart. When children are surrounded by affectionate huggers, they are more likely to grow up to be affectionate huggers themselves.

Teenagers

No matter what their tribe—Goth, rocker, blader, boarder, preppy, punk, gamer—thousands of teenagers have come to me for hugs. In fact they seem to crave hugs more then any other age group. Again and again they have said to me, "This is the best hug I've gotten in my life!" Then, as Oliver Twist might say, they ask, "Please, sir, can I have some more?" I have heard these sentiments expressed countless times both by homeless youths and by teens with stable home lives. Most teenagers who hug me are very respectful, and express their gratitude with a level of sincerity that adults generally can't seem to find. I see many, many people from all walks of life who, I am sorry to say, are touch-starved, affection-hungry and thirsty for love, and teens are by far the most famished. It seems to me that there is a definite lack of affectionate touch in the lives of many of these wonderful kids.

Over the past decade much research has been done on how therapeutic or affectionate touch affects behaviour in teenagers. One study suggests that teens, both male and female, who include physical interaction in their social communication skills—like touching, hugging or holding hands—are less prone to aggression and violent behaviour than those who don't. Another concludes that teens who received chair massages twice a week for a month became less aggressive. In a world of escalating violence and aggression, it might be worthy to note this correlation between physical affection and aggression. We all need to be touched and feel loved, especially those in our society who are living through the physical and psychological transition from childhood to adulthood.

I watched a father try to enthusiastically hug his teenage sons, who both reacted with extreme discomfort. I witnessed a mother's cynicism as she brushed off her older child's attempt at giving her a hug as being silly and childish. I saw a daughter shy away from a family hug, calling it gross. These are just some examples of the uncomfortable situations between parents and teens that transpire before me every day. I am certain that many parents are saddened and hurt by the uneasiness that many teens feel about showing physical affection towards them, and the reverse is equally true. I have also noticed that often, hugs shared between parents and teens are given in a habitual or even dismissive manner, as if it was a necessary chore like taking the dog for a walk.

As adult members of society, are we not role models to the younger generations? If we, as adults, express discomfort with an affectionate hug, how then do we expect our children to grow up to be physically affectionate adults themselves? It's no wonder that so many youths and adults alike find my hugs so special and comforting. I put my heart into hugging them… I just wish more people did the same.

"You are such an inspiration to people like me, 16-year-olds who need to make crucial life decisions but who are so intimidated by this big wide world that the thought of 'a future' is overwhelming. We're bombarded with absurd notions that success only comes to those who are doctors, lawyers or scientists; that creativity and self-fulfillment are not worth 'wasting your life over.' But you're living proof to me that making your dream a reality is anything but a waste. From hugging you this summer and then hearing you on the radio (and even seeing you on television) it's become even clearer to me that people with your confidence and imagination are what make the world go around! More of us should be like you, because you instil happiness and greatness in everyone who meets you. Your success is marked by the smiles you put on peoples' faces, and that by far surpasses any so-called 'noble' job that I know of."

- Danya K., Quebec, Canada

Every job, infused with the right intention, has the potential to be noble, just as every adult is a potential role model to a child or teenager. What matters is not the role you fill, but how you do what you do. Youths need to witness real-life examples of different types of success, different lifestyles, different ways of thinking and different beliefs. This shows them the range of possibilities that life can offer them. They need models to help them fulfill their own potential and to help them believe that their future can also be beautiful, meaningful and abundant.

The Disabled

The physically and mentally disabled of our society are just as much, if not more, in need of human affection then those of us who are able-bodied and sound of mind. Yet many of us are hesitant to offer an affectionate hug to an incapacitated member of our society for a variety of reasons—discomfort, fear, judgment, even ignorance. The first few times a wheelchair-bound person stopped before me, I too was hesitant to offer them a hug. I thought they would think that I was singling them out for affection because of their disability, and would be offended. I quickly realized that these were my own discomforts expressing themselves and that in truth my invitation would be not only welcome but deeply appreciated. I knew that if my desire to give affection was sincere and heartfelt, which it was, then I needn't worry about how my offer would be received. Even if they refused I was certain that my gesture was appreciated. If you have the urge to hug someone, the kind of body or mind they have should not matter.

It is always a special moment for me to embrace a disabled person, as it always seems to be a special moment for them as well. Often, at about the third breath, they will begin to giggle and giggle, of course this makes me giggle as well and together we end our hug in cheerful laughter. I have asked several of my wheelchair-bound hugging regulars why they always giggle when I hug them. Their answers were surprisingly similar; being suddenly filled with happy joyful energy made them giddy and giggly. Knowing that my actions bring delight to another being who is struggling with the reality of their life is powerfully motivating for me as it gives me the courage to continue on my quest to bring joy to my world one hug at a time.

Every single one of us is a feeling, breathing, living being of God, each with our own limitations and life challenges. That some of those challenges are more obvious than others does not make a difference. Each of us plays an integral role in the evolution of our society; we all have an honoured and rightful place in this world, so to forget, reject or ignore any one person who does not seem whole in our eyes is to dishonour our own imperfect self. We all deserve to be touched by the love of others as often as possible. So I encourage you to offer your tender touch to someone, not disabled but simply differently abled than you, whenever you get the chance.

The Elderly

The Hugger Busker is regularly invited to give hugs at health and wellness events and retirement centres for the elderly. When I first arrive at a centre dressed in my elegant period suit, I cut a striking figure, looking very much like a dapper man from the residents' youth. My presence incites curiosity and excitement as the residents have been forewarned of my arrival. Throughout the day many will come to see me to chat, share a hug or just watch. Some are grumpy, others sprightly, others sad, and some fierce. All will hesitate before approaching, checking me out to make certain that I am genuine. The moment they realize that my intentions are kind they will approach and sighing deeply, they will let me embrace them lovingly. Many tell me that their families rarely visit and that the last tender hug they shared was with their dearly departed spouse. For some it has been months, for others years. To not be held affectionately in someone's arms for five, ten, fifteen years... I can't begin to imagine what that must be like. As my day ends and I prepare to leave, the question most asked is, "When will you be back to hug us again?"

To be hugged, to be touched affectionately with care and love, is a deep need for the aged in our society. Many are mere shadows of their former selves, lonely and forgotten, sometimes by choice but more often by circumstance. Though their bodies are crumbling and their faculties are diminishing, their hearts remain youthful and their spirits alive. We should not let them go so easily, these beautiful men and women, whose past struggles and successes have paved the way for the technological and social advantages that we, the younger generations, take for granted today.

We who are surrounded by family and loved ones should make it a point to search out people who are lonely, abandoned and forgotten, and offer them a moment of companionship and of tender affection, a moment that will be cherished in their hearts for the remainder of their days—because for some it really is a question of days. There are numerous organizations that need volunteers to regularly spend time with seniors for shopping, walking, visiting, entertaining or just sit with them and listen. The stories, experiences and wisdom that someone who has lived 70, 80 or 90 years has to share are just amazing. Just go to the park on a nice day and start talking to the old man feeding the pigeons or the wizened woman picking up discarded plastic bags and cans. Share a conversation with them and then offer them a hug... you may discover that the life you are holding in your arms is much more precious then you had ever imagined.

Pets and Animal Friends

Oh, how we love the furry, woolly, feathery, scaly beings that enliven our homes and bring unconditional love into our lives! Our cherished pets are by our side when we need companionship, comfort and protection; they even seem to sense our moods, cozying up when we are feeling sad, or playful and affectionate when we're happy. They listen to us endlessly without ever interrupting. Creatures of comfort can be amazing to have in our lives!

Pets enrich our lives in countless ways with their unconditional affection and undemanding presence. It is a fact that animal companionship brings many wonderful benefits to human owners; for children and the elderly these benefits are even greater. Studies reveal that children who have dogs growing up tend to be more self-confident and responsible adults. Caring for a pet teaches responsibility and nurturance, and the unconditional love and companionship that the child experiences in return builds feelings of self-worth and confidence. For many elderly people who live alone and have a hard time getting about to socialize, it is the same; pets bring much-needed companionship, loving affection, and protection to their daily lives, and help them live longer, healthier and happier.

In order to earn our pets' loyalty and lifelong friendship we must take responsibility for their care and well-being; at a minimum, we must provide food, shelter and loving attention. There are a variety of ways to give loving affection to our pets, and hugging is only one of them. Domesticated animals need to be held, loved and appreciated. Just like humans, physical affection and touching plays an important role in their emotional and psychological well-being.

Just one word of warning: Don't hug or pet an animal who doesn't know you without asking its owner, and letting it get comfortable with your scent and your presence before touching it. It will let you know if it wants your touch; if you don't want to get bitten, don't insist against clear signs of rejection. Respect, the first principle of hugging, applies to animals as well.

Teddy Bears and Cuddly Comforts

Linus, with his ever-present blanket, represents all those children and adults who find reassurance and calm in the presence of their favourite blanky, teddy, doll, or pillow. For some, these cuddly soothers are emotional or psychological crutches that reflect deep fears or insecurities; for others they are simply habitual practices that continue to bring immediate physical comfort and a sense of security and companionship. Two cuddly soothers that have brought comfort to my life are the hugging pillow and the teddy bear.

The hugging pillow is a pillow the length of two and a half regular ones, so it can be hugged with the arms and legs simultaneously. My hugging pillow has come in handy over the years. Not only has it comforted me through more then a few lonely nights, but its regular use, after a car accident, helped to readjust my sleeping posture and relieve me of recurring neck and back pains. I also find it very satisfying to spend a few hours in my hammock, sipping hot cocoa and reading a good book while curled up next to the downy warmth of this large huggable pillow.

The teddy bear is more then a century old. Created almost simultaneously in the USA and Germany, its name remains distinctly American, named after the man who inspired its creation and the teddy bear craze that followed—President Theodore "Teddy" Roosevelt. Since then, animals, characters and creatures both real and fantastical have graced the beds of countless children throughout the world. Whether they're plush or ragged, miniature or gigantic, these cuddly sources of comfort keep us feeling secure and cozy.

My sister has a large collection of cuddly creatures from childhood that she drags out of storage every few years to spread all over her bedroom. It is wonderful to see her indulge in such a playful and childlike pastime. As the little girl emerges, the woman becomes enlivened and filled with a youthful energy that magically lights up her eyes. She becomes radiant and beautiful when the loving, joyful innocence of her inner child emerges.

Country fairs and carnivals are full of skill-testing booths that give away stuffed toys of every shape and size to lucky winners. When I was ten years old my dad took me to one of these carnivals where he proceeded to win me a stuffed toy. I felt was so proud and happy that my dad had won me such a prize. It was a long green snake, and it quickly found its way into my sister's collection. Years later I was thrilled and proud when I won my new girl a big yellow rabbit on our first date; though the relationship never flourished, that moment remains a memorable one for me.

Apart from these two experiences I am a late bloomer when it comes to truly appreciating the comfort of cuddly toys.

The Christmas after I began hugging, I surprised Jade by buying each of us a teddy bear. She named her bear Ruma, the loving one, and mine is called Rumi, the silent one. Now whenever I take a power nap, Rumi is always there to cuddle with as I journey into my dreams and beyond. Simply put cuddly comforts are for everyone who is a kid at heart.

Hugging in Strange Lands

In the West, we are used to naturally expressing our affection freely and without restraint if the mood takes us. Every culture is different in their approach and tolerance of public displays of affection. What is comfortable behaviour in one society may cause discomfort and even be seen as disrespect to those from other cultures.

In most Western cultures it is more frequent to see two women hug, or a man and a woman hug, than to see two men do so. But there are exceptions; in

Italy and Greece, for example, it is normal behaviour for groups of young men to walk around town together arm-in-arm, holding hands, touching and hugging.

In India, Pakistan and most Middle Eastern countries, one is more apt to see two men hugging in public then two women, and rarely will you see a man and a woman touch in public, let alone hug. In fact in many of these countries religious or social mores strongly disapprove of public displays of affection between the sexes. It is not only frowned upon, but in many cases punishable by law, with punishments ranging from hefty fines to much worse—being jailed, being beaten, being ostracized from the family or community, and in some rare cases, being set upon and killed in the name of family honour.

When traveling to Middle Eastern or Asian countries, especially if you plan a honeymoon or romantic getaway, please look into the social mores and laws governing public displays of affection before you depart. It might be very disappointing to find out once there that holding hands, kissing, hugging and so forth are disallowed and may get you in trouble, even if you are a Westerner. Respect the traditions of the culture or country in which you are a guest and you will have a much more pleasant trip. If all else fails, you may want to refer to page 178 and perfect your Air Hugging technique!

Awareness in Hugging

As a public hugger, one of my biggest challenges is dealing with people's mistrust of strangers and the fear brought on by unfamiliar situations. In spite of the fact that I promote heartfelt hugging as an acceptable and even indispensable practice in any environment, the reality of our world today is such that one must remain aware of the limitations dictated by our social and professional mores.

The sexualization of our society through the promotion and commercialization of sex and sensuality has reached such a saturation point that one cannot walk by a bus stop without being stroked by the allure of desire or lust. So it is not surprising that men and women are careful to keep their shows of physical affection to a minimum with each other, and even with children, for fear that their intentions will be perceived as something other then innocent affection. Society as a whole has become overly sensitive about any kind of touching or physical contact, which is too easily interpreted as a sexual overture or even as sexual harassment. Be especially careful in the workplace, where, apart from a handshake or pat on the back, shows of physical affection may be considered inappropriate.

Keep the following suggestions in mind when hugging someone who is not in your intimate circle. Consider them, adapt them, or create your own, as you are the best judge of what is suitable for your hugging enjoyment.

1. Be courteous; always ask before hugging someone, or their children or pets.

2. Unless a child offers you a hug first, always ask for their permission.

3. When someone wants to end the hug and pulls away from your embrace, even if it only lasted three seconds, let them go!

4. Don't let your hands wander. Keep them on the person's upper back, either firmly placed on the back or gently patting the back.

5. When hugging a woman, men would do best to keep their body, from the chest down, apart from hers. No matter how appealing this might sound, gentlemen, do not hold a woman so tightly that her breasts push into your chest. These are to be heartfelt hugs, not heart-stopping hugs.

6. When hugging a man, women should be friendly and casual. Do not linger, as men tend to easily interpret a lingering feminine touch as being flirtatious and inviting. Keep your body, from the breasts down, apart from his.

- 3 -

THE FIVE PRINCIPLES
OF HUGGING

1. Hug with Respect!

*Every person's ability and willingness to express physical
intimacy is different. By respecting your limits and those
of your hugging partner, you honour each other and you
honour the beauty of your humanity.*

To respect means to show consideration for
someone, to hold them worthy of esteem. If we are to
respect others, we must begin by respecting ourselves.
By showing consideration for our own needs and
limits, by holding ourselves worthy of esteem in spite
of our human imperfections, we learn to be more
accepting of ourselves and in turn more loving. It's
much easier to tolerate and show compassion for

others when we ourselves understand how difficult it can be to remain kind, caring and considerate human beings. I often remind myself that even if someone's behaviour does not merit respect, I must still respect them as an individual. Our shared human condition and the spirit of God within us make us both worthy of that respect and compassion.

None of us are of greater or lesser value than anyone else. By accepting our imperfections we can come to appreciate and even love the complexity of our human condition, and through that we can find the grace to respect the uniqueness of others, whether we agree with their perceptions of life or not. To respect people is to honour those differences.

When it comes to sharing the physical and emotional intimacy of a hug, it is vital to be attentive to your hugging partner's limits and to respect them. When inviting someone into your arms, simply ask yourself how they are receiving your embrace. Are they tense and awkward, anxious and shifty, unresponsive and stiff, nervous and giggly? By intuitively listening to how their physical body reacts to yours, you will learn a great deal about how they are emotionally experiencing this moment of intimacy. If your partner wants to pull away after a few seconds, give them a brief squeeze to let them know it's okay and then gently let them go, even if you would have preferred a longer embrace. Just the fact that you were receptive to their unspoken needs or fears will make them feel more secure and willing to hug you again at another time. Also, if someone doesn't want a hug, accept their refusal with a smile. You never know what emotional or physical response a hug can bring out in someone, or why they are reacting the way they do, so don't judge and never take it personally.

Though it is important to remain attentive to your partner, you must never forget to listen to your own needs and respond to them accordingly. When you are the one in need of a little tender loving care, let yourself accept the love that a hug can offer. On the other hand, if you feel uncomfortable or uneasy in an embrace, then you must respect yourself by acknowledging these feelings and acting appropriately. You may want to gently disengage from the embrace with gratitude in your heart and kindness in your smile, or you may choose instead to surrender to the loving intention of the hug, trusting that life never puts you in a situation that you aren't ready to handle. Regardless of your choice, make sure you choose sincerely, and from a place of respect.

2. Hug without Conditions!

Like love itself, a hug must be unconditional for it to be deeply meaningful. When you give freely from the heart, without expectations, you invariably receive far more then you would ever have imagined.

A hug is a beautiful, generous act of unconditional love and kindness shared between two or more human beings. Give your hugs with only the other's pleasure in mind, irrespective of whether they show appreciation or have something to give in return. The joy that you receive from sharing your love with another and the pleasure that they receive from your gesture is what hugging without condition is all about.

To hug is also to receive this delightful gift from another without feeling that you must give something in return. When you accept someone's gift of love wholeheartedly, without obligation, you honour it best!

I have discovered that when I expect a return for my love I am most often disappointed, as my expectations are never met. The sweetness of the moment is spoiled by the bitterness of my silent yearning for reciprocity. When I expect my pound for pound, I always end up cutting into my own heart to satisfy my selfish cravings. The sages of our time and times past speak of the universal truth of giving and receiving, they teach us that one should sow what one wishes to reap. It took me years to transform the wisdom of this simple yet powerful truth from intellectual understanding into personal knowledge.

Through my hugging, the realization came that if I gave to others what I needed most, the Universe would fulfill my every need. The more I gave freely from my heart, without expectations, the more I received.

3. Hug with Heart!

Every hug is, to one degree or another, the physical manifestation of Divine love. If your intention when hugging is a purely loving one, then your spirit will be lifted up; comfort and joy will fill the hearts of everyone who shares your embrace.

There are so many physical variations of hugging that it's impossible to name one as better than another. A quick but deeply sincere pat on the back, at the right moment, can have a momentous impact on the one receiving it, where as a crushing bear hug, devoid of genuine feeling, can leave someone shaken and mistrustful.

So if it isn't the outward form that makes for a profound hugging experience, then what does? Simply, the difference is in your inner intention.

Intention is defined as an aim, or a strong purpose that guides an action. Every action we take in life is directed by inner intention, whether that intention is conscious or intuitive, selfish or sincere. This means that we have the power to choose the intentions that guide the nature of our actions. We deal with many events in our lives in a reactive and unconscious way, which makes it difficult to identify our intentions, let alone control them. But when we give a hug, we can consciously choose what qualities our embrace carries with it. The transformative power of hugging is not so much in the physical act of the hug as in the inner intention brought to it. Imagine, if you will, that the intention you have towards another person is like a vibration that emerges from you and is received by them. If your hugging intention is a loving one, your partner will feel your comfort, care, concern and love without any words being spoken.

The next time you take someone into your arms, fill your heart with the desire to love and then let that intention fill your embrace. With every breath, silently say in your heart's mind, "be filled with love," "be comforted," "be joyful," or whatever you feel they most need at the moment. Trust your intuition. Inner intention is powerful, whether in hugging or in life; if used wisely, it can bring about profound transformation and healing. By making the intention of every hug you share truly loving you will not only find yourself uplifted, but you will also bring joy, comfort and healing to all those you embrace.

4. Hug with Gratitude!

A hug is a beautiful, life-affirming expression of our humanity. It is through this simple yet profound gesture that gratitude and reverence for the sacredness of life can be expressed and honoured.

Whether we recognize it or not, life continuously provides us with countless opportunities for growth and abundance. Many of these opportunities come to us during our daily interactions with others. Each of these interactions offers us a chance to embrace our human condition and in doing so, to improve it. Of course, that means our opportunities for gratitude are also limitless. To offer gratitude is a noble act of humility and grace. This act holds the power to raise us above the mundane pettiness of day-to-day affairs. To offer gratitude is to affirm the generous spirit of human nature while honouring the greater glory of God as the source and substance of all our good. It's essential to be thankful and show gratitude for what life has and will afford us if we want our deepest desires to manifest in reality.

Thankfulness can be expressed in countless ways. It can be silently spoken in the heart, for example while praying or meditating. It can be an extravagant affair of flowers and song, or a warm handshake, or a few appreciative words written in a card, or simply a faint smile and nod. Appreciation well intended is always appreciated in turn. We all like knowing that our actions or simply our presence has brought satisfaction to another, so why not give others the same kind of appreciation that we enjoy receiving?

Every day we pass up many opportunities to show our gratitude to others. Look around you. Who deserves your gratitude today? A loved one for loving you, a co-worker for their support, a stranger for their unsolicited kindness? So what's keeping you? Screw up your courage and go tell them, or better yet, show them. How about with a hug? If it feels right, go for it. Every hug you give is the perfect opportunity to express your gratitude. If you hug with gratitude, people will in turn be grateful that you did.

5. Hug the Moment!

Every hug, and every person you hug, deserves your complete and undivided attention. In this moment of Divine sharing, take the time to be fully present and mindful.
This is your life, right now!
So breathe it, enjoy it, appreciate it, embrace it and share it!

The only place you can ever physically be is here! The only time that you can ever be anyplace is now! No matter where your mind wanders off to, you always are and always will be here, now. Whether you fully experience the present moment is up to you. Truly, what could really be more important or pressing then what you are experiencing at this very instant?

How often do you lose yourself in meandering thoughts, unsubstantiated worries, fantastical imaginings or reflective reveries? More often then not, we disappear somewhere into the recesses of our mind and go through the motions of being present without ever being aware of it. We tend to live quantity time and not quality time.

Every single moment of this life is precious, meaningful, and worthy of our attention. Every single moment presents you with an opportunity to live with respect, with unconditional love, with heartfelt intention, and with sincere gratitude. Just let the moment unfold!

As you begin to savour each moment as you would a rare delicacy, you might also want to consider how equally precious the individuals who bring guidance and meaning to your journey are. No matter what role someone plays in the adventure of your life, cherish their presence; they are your guides and travel companions. When you hug someone, do so with mindful awareness, relishing each moment of the hug. Revel in it, take delight in every last detail of it: the approach, the generosity of spirit, the physical intimacy, the emotional investment, the shared breath, the rhythm of beating hearts, the warmth of another human being. This is a moment of Divine sharing, so take the time to be fully present in it— breathe it, enjoy it, appreciate it, show gratitude for it and embrace it as if it were your last!

Hugging is the language of the heart;
utterly Divine yet absolutely human!

- 4 -

THE TREASURY OF HUGS

Welcome to the treasury of hugs! Here you will find a collection of hugs, each as expressive and delightfully human as the next. A hug is a unique and precious gift that holds the potential to create lasting solidarity, profound intimacy, joyful celebration and healing of body, mind and spirit.

This is not, by any means, an authoritative list of hugs, but rather a collection of personal thoughts, observations and experiences on the diversity and artfulness of this most human experience.

Though I have named and categorized my hugs, I wish to make it clear that this is intended as neither a judgment nor a characterization of the people who have had the courage to share a hug with me. Nor should you judge yourself or others if you recognize yours or someone else's style in a given description, but rather take this opportunity to explore new ways of sharing the tender touch of human intimacy. Each individual brings their own personal style and energy to every hug they give, so when hugging, keep in mind that the true value of a hug lays in the inner intention inhabiting it, rather then the physical expression of it. Please use these descriptions as a light-hearted guide to the many ways in which we humans express and share our caring, concern and delight through hugging.

May these gems bring a sparkle to your life and the lives of the people you share them with!

Basic Hugs

There are three basic physical forms of hugging of which most of the hugs in this treasury are variants: the A-Frame, the Formal and the Wrapping.

THE A-FRAME

Do you want to connect with a lot of flair, but don't want to get too close either physically or emotionally? Then this might be perfect for you. It's not that the people involved don't like or care about each other. But either the social situation or their personal habits call for a quick, casual, showy greeting. This is called the A-Frame because when the hug is formed it looks just like an uppercase A.

1. Stand a few feet from person you will hug.

2. Keep the legs wide and straight.

3. Bend the upper chest forward at the hips. This will naturally push the backside out behind.

4. Hold the other person's hands, upper arms or shoulders to maintain balance.

5. Kiss or pretend to kiss each other's cheeks.

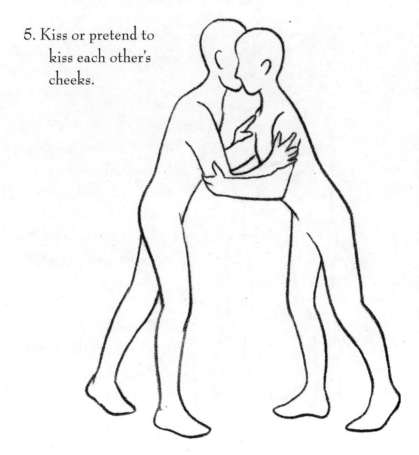

THE FORMAL

For occasions that demand reserve, decorum and formality, or for individuals who are naturally stiff and uncomfortable with overt shows of physical affection, the Formal offers distinction and distance.

1. Stand a foot or so from the person you will hug.

2. Keep the legs and body straight.

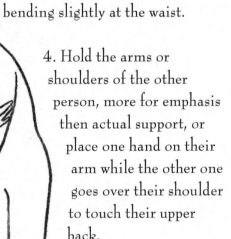

3. Lean your body forward, bending slightly at the waist.

4. Hold the arms or shoulders of the other person, more for emphasis then actual support, or place one hand on their arm while the other one goes over their shoulder to touch their upper back.

5. Kiss the person's cheek, or pat their back a few times.

THE WRAPPING

Like a beautiful wrapper around a delectable sweet, this form is the basis of all the healing and comforting hugs in the Treasury. This hug invites you to express the warmth of your heart while wrapping yourself in the experience of a shared embrace.

1. Stand very close to the person you will hug.

2. Lean forward from the waist and bring your chest to theirs.

3. Wrap your arms around their shoulders or torso.

4. Place your palms on their back.

5. Hold them against you.

Casual Hugs

The casual hug is a cordial and friendly greeting that is somewhat impersonal, and lacking in physical or emotional intimacy. Most of us do not have the time, the inclination or the energy to greet everyone we meet with a full-bodied heartfelt embrace, nor is it always appropriate to do so. It's interesting to note how varied a casual hug can be depending on the social or emotional implications that surround it. Your intention, or lack thereof, also plays an important part in how this hug is delivered, but most importantly, how it's received. The following casual hugs are the most common ones in use today. Although they may be somewhat dispassionate, it might be helpful to keep the third principle, "hugging with heart," in mind when you find yourself participating in one. By simply adding a little sincere loving to the casualness of these embraces, you can make a world of difference!

KISSY-KISSY HUG – Classification: A-Frame

I first discovered this charming hug in the early '90s' when I lived in Paris. I had originally named it the Parisian Hug because of the frequency with which my Parisian friends used it. But since it's an equally common greeting among Quebecois and Latin cultures, it seemed more appropriate to give it a physically descriptive designation rather then a cultural one.

When used casually, much like a handshake, this perfunctory kissing of the cheeks gives people the impression of being on intimate terms with one another without actually being an intimate act whatsoever. In fact there is often such a lack of conviction in its use that in many cases it has become an automatic gesture, much like when we ask "How are you?" without much sincerity or interest in a real answer.

The Kissy-Kissy Hug is a quick embrace highlighted by several kisses on the cheeks. In perfect A-Frame fashion the individuals will bend forward and will simultaneously kiss each other's cheeks once, twice, even three times. This is a fast, active hug often performed in the midst of a lot of cheerful chatter. Despite its growing potential for insincerity, this hug can be given with a wonderful

quality of cheerfulness, warmth and camaraderie, especially when it's infused with the authentic pleasure of greeting someone. It's a hug frequently used at school reunions, weddings, funerals, and other social gatherings.

COURTEOUS HUG – Classification: Formal

During my 20-year career as a film and television actor and as a branch president of ACTRA, the national film actor's union, I have attended numerous movie premieres and swanky formal events where I

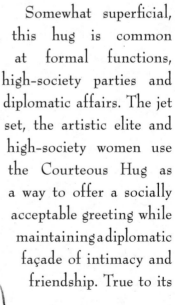

have witnessed and politely enjoyed many Courteous Hugs.

Somewhat superficial, this hug is common at formal functions, high-society parties and diplomatic affairs. The jet set, the artistic elite and high-society women use the Courteous Hug as a way to offer a socially acceptable greeting while maintaining a diplomatic façade of intimacy and friendship. True to its name, it is a show of courtesy, nothing more and nothing less.

While the typical Formal Hug is stiff and proper in nature, it has the potential to be quite elegant and dignified. Both parties will lean forward slightly and lightly touch each other's cheeks while kissing the air nearby.

Apart from the setting it could be that one or both parties are uncomfortable with expressing physical affection. Personal, cultural or social conditioning often dictates how individuals deal with public displays of physical affection, so if you come across someone who shows discomfort or lack of sincerity when hugging you, don't take it personally; be understanding and gentle in your approach.

PATTING HUG – Classification: A-Frame

This seemingly genuine hug exudes false sincerity and detachment. It gives the illusion of being comforting, but that in fact offers little to anyone in real need of comfort or consolation. I like to believe that when someone approaches me for a hug it is because they want to share an authentic moment of tenderness with me. So when a person drapes their arms over my shoulders like a pair of soggy noodles, and lamely pats my back, saying in a tone of simulated concern, "Aw, poor you, you look so lonely," or "Hey, it's okay, buddy, here's your hug," it saddens me that they need to dissimulate to hug. Why pretend to be caring and compassionate when your intention is not? On the other hand, if it makes someone happy to believe they are hugging me solely for my benefit, I really don't mind; I know, and they know, that they are receiving the warmth and comfort that they have been craving.

But any person in real need of consolation will feel the lack of conviction in the hug, and unfortunately it might aggravate their suffering rather then comfort it. As a hugger yourself, this is when you need to remember principle number 1 – hug with respect. Remember to meet the person where they are and reach out to them with sincerity, even if you can feel they're not entirely ready to do the same.

When someone needs to find an excuse to give a hug, it's usually because they themselves are in need of one, whether they admit it or not.

MANLY HUG – Classification: Formal

This is a masculine greeting that seems more prevalent among Latin, Slavic and Arab men. Movies have often portrayed this hug as the stereotypical greeting of Arab sheiks and mobsters, but that doesn't mean you won't see a father send his daughter off to college or a son off to war in this manner. The Manly Hug can be a sign of respect or courtesy between people with a lengthy allegiance that stops short of friendship, or it can be used to express deep affection or love in a very restrained, masculine manner.

When it's not infused with deep respect or genuine affection, this hug remains stiff, dry and even mildly menacing. The manly hug is not shared equally; there is a very subtle hierarchy at play here. Generally, the man who initiates the embrace will place his hands firmly on the other's shoulders, establishing dominance and denoting a higher social, familial or financial status, while the receiver remains physically passive.

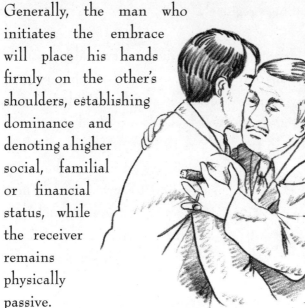

The hugger will then lean close for a short embrace or simply to kiss the other's cheek. He will then release his grip and allow the other to step back. If a strong emotion overtakes the hugger, he may pull the person back into his arms for a longer and tighter embrace... or he may simply stifle his emotions and do nothing.

When I was thirteen my parents decided to send me on a study trip to Europe for a month; it was my first time travelling abroad. I remember standing at the departure gate in my purple velvet suit being sent off by Mom and Dad. The Manly Hug was exactly the kind of hug my father gave me, loving yet formally stiff and emotionally restrained. Since coming to watch me give free hugs he has become much more relaxed in his hugging style and now enjoys sharing heartfelt hugs regularly.

HAND CLASP HUG – Classification: Formal/Wrapping

Groups of young men from tough neighbourhoods regularly stop to check me out when I'm hugging in the public square. Weighed down by gold chains and drowning in the coolness of baggy designer clothing, they joke about getting hugs, but none usually dare to approach me. There is a very strong level of machismo and insecurity running through these neighbourhood posses, who wear their bravado like a coat of armour.

When I offer a hug, most of these guys laugh and immediately back away from me. The bolder ones of the bunch might offer to clasp my hand or lay on a high five. One young man once clasped my hand, pulled me strongly towards him, trapping our hands between our chests, and slapped me on the back. Upon releasing me he said, "This is how *we* do it."

This clasping of hands, banging of chests and slapping of backs was infused with machismo. It was how these youths expressed their affection and camaraderie for each other. Different groups I've encountered have had different cool handshakes that they like to incorporate upon releasing the hand clasp. Over time I've learned several slick moves from these kids; it's been a lot of fun to jive with them.

This type of hug is not just for street gangs; many athletes use the "cool dude" Hand Clasp Hug as a show of brotherly affection and support, especially with their team-mates. Just watch any team sporting or athletic event and you'll see a whole variety of them.

SIDE-BY-SIDE HUG — Classification: Wrapping

When I stand next to my loved one as we hold each other silently, we share a moment filled with beauty and serenity. But the true nature of this hug is revealed not in stillness but in motion. The Side-by-Side is the perfect hug for Sunday walks, moonlight talks, window-shopping and museum-hopping. Casual, meandering, playful and relaxing, this embrace is a sign of romantic closeness, friendship or camaraderie. Depending on culture and sexual orientation, you will see gender matches of all kinds wandering the streets this way in most Western cities.

In the public square, I see many pairs and trios walk by me side-by-side, with arms around each other's waists or shoulders, or a combination of the two. The more romantic duos seem to let their hands teasingly

wander up and down again. Girlfriends are often more touchy-feely with each other; while not being flirty, they may be more playfully intimate in how they hold onto each other. Male friends will, on the other hand, usually stay within two variations: arms around each other's shoulders or arm-in-arm. The hands generally never wander, unless they are more than friends.

As for me, I have always enjoyed midnight strolls by the water's edge with my partner; it's a perfect time to unwind and reconnect. As for my male friends, I especially like walking arm-over-shoulder with them, especially when discussing personal issues. It makes for deeper listening and strengthens the bond of friendship.

Dynamic Hugs

Running, jumping, leaping, lifting, twirling or fighting, these hugs are physically active and intensely emotional. It's this combination that makes them so dynamic and beautiful to witness or participate in. The need for emotional expression on the part of the person initiating the hug is so immediate, so compelling, that it manifests itself in a dramatic physical form.

Spontaneous in nature, these hugs usually take both parties completely by surprise. There are two variations to this dynamic: either a rapidly growing build of energy that suddenly ignites, such as when a person sees a long-lost friend, runs toward them and leaps into their arms; or, an unexpected spontaneous explosion of movement, like when one person suddenly grabs another and lifts them up. All but one of these hugs are candid expressions of joyful exuberance and deep affection. Only the Warrior's Hug, used in martial combat, stands apart from all the other hugs in the treasury in that it is highly aggressive, fierce and tactical in nature.

RUNNING HUG – Classification: Wrapping

Children and passionately romantic lovers seem to take great delight in this beautiful expression of joy. Though it is primarily young people who indulge in this hug, sometimes adults who are not lovers are adventurous enough to follow the whims of their inner child.

Totally spontaneous in nature, this hug is often inspired by the appearance of a cherished friend or loved one—though in my case, the people who've chosen to dash into my waiting embrace seemed to be inspired by the sheer pleasure of sharing a free and heartfelt hug. It's such a joy to see someone abandon all pretence and form to satisfy the pleasure of their heart! Propelled by a burst of gleeful exuberance, eyes sparkling with laughter, people have sprinted towards me and launched themselves into my welcoming arms for an all-embracing hug. So much uninhibited playfulness, warmth and appreciation embodies these hugs that I am often left beaming and giddy for hours after.

As for lovers, there is usually more anticipation and emotional build-up to this hug. As they collide with each other, one person will often break the momentum of the other's run by lifting the person off the ground and twirling them around. This romantic romp will usually end in a consuming kiss. (For more on romance and hugging, read the Intimate Hugs section!)

A Note of Caution:

Unless the runner is much smaller or lighter than the receiver of the hug, I strongly suggest that the runner slow down just before contact. It's just no fun if the recipient of your energetic embrace is knocked over or injured. The receiver might want to place their strongest leg behind them, and lean forward slightly while bending at the knees to more easily absorb the momentum of the runner. If room allows, they can twirl around together at the moment of contact to avoid losing balance.

REUNION HUG — Classification: Wrapping

Every day, the world's train stations, bus depots and airports are the site of this emotionally charged, joyful hug. Sometimes cheerful, sometimes tearful, sometimes gregarious, sometimes sober, but always heartfelt, this is a hug for old friends, lonely lovers or cherished relatives who are reuniting after a long (or seemingly long!) time apart.

Sometimes when I travel, I see a welcoming party of one or more awaiting the arrival of a much-loved traveler, with anticipation bubbling visibly. Between bouts of excited chatter and hopeful exclamations of false sightings, their eyes search hopefully through the passing crowd. Then, on the other side of the gate appears the weary, baggage-laden traveler, who is hurrying along in the

GATE 3B

hopes of finding comfort of heart and peace of mind in the company of loved ones. Suddenly, through the weaving throng, the moment of recognition arrives. The eyes lock, the excitement rises, the pace quickens and with a surge of exhilaration the traveler emerges a few steps from the welcoming committee. The traveler drops their bags to the ground and swiftly merges into the waiting happy embrace. With eyes closed and arms tightly wrapped around each other they may sway a bit from side to side. After a moment they pull apart slightly to look at each other, as if to say, "Yes, it really is you!" The emotions flow, with a potent mix of kisses, laughter, tears, more hugging, more excitement, and the touching of hands, backs and faces. This can go on for quite some time, especially if there are many family members eagerly waiting to share in the hug.

One thing I've frequently seen in airports is the scene of a woman giving an enthusiastic hug, and kicking her heels back with a gleeful yelp at the moment she is lifted up off the ground by her friend or lover at the moment of the embrace, making for a joyful and memorable "Kodak moment". Like many tall or large people surely do, I sometimes wish I were smaller and lighter, so I could kick up my heels too once in a while!

LEAPING HUG – Classification: Wrapping

There are times when life offers us the most amazing moments. Sometimes, incredible news or an unexpected event brings us out of our staid selves with a leap of ecstatic joy, and we're overcome with a bursting desire to express profound gratitude to everyone around us with kisses and hugs. The Leaping Hug is the unrestrained celebration of one of these moments—like winning the national lottery or scoring the winning goal. Though this hug is as spontaneous as the previous two, it is usually initiated at close range. Often letting out a shriek of delight, the leaper will jump up into the arms of the unsuspecting person closest to them and wrap their arms and legs around their body. Ideally, the recipient of such a dynamic hug is strong enough, agile enough and playful enough to help make it the momentous moment it's intended to be!

A Note of Caution:

Unlike the running hug, the leaping hug is often unexpected. So be certain that the person you are leaping on is capable of catching you. Otherwise you will both find yourselves flat on the ground crying in pain rather than in joy. This has happened to me on several occasions—professional hazard I suppose! Keep it safe and fun for everyone.

BEAR HUG – Classification: Wrapping

This is the most physically powerful of all hugs, generally used by bear-like men with strong, large physiques to show either deep affection and camaraderie or aggressive physical dominance. It is also a fighting technique used in several martial arts; this will be discussed in the Warrior's Hug section. For now I'll focus on the friendlier nature of this embrace.

The larger person wraps their arms around the smaller person's body, from either the front of the back, and squeezes them tightly, maybe even shaking than from side to side or lifting them off the ground. Sometimes the airborne person will be twirled around once or twice. I have received many Bear Hugs and I find them to be wonderfully liberating; I just allow myself to let go and enjoy the ride. I'll hold on, open my legs wide, throw my head back, and make like I am flying. What a thrill! A good Bear Hug always makes me laugh and leaves me feeling energized and tension-free.

Sometimes when I see a big man who is hesitant to hug me, I'll ask him if he would indulge me in a Bear Hug. Rarely do they refuse, and they always leave cheerful. I will admit that at the moment of lift-off, a hint of panic sometimes passes through me, but it quickly dissipates as I surrender to the playfully affectionate spirit of the moment.

A Note of Caution:

Before you go off Bear-Hugging all your friends, remember that it's best not to try giving one to someone taller or heavier than you; the physical dynamics won't work, and you may cause yourself back injury and embarrassment. If it's a Bear Hug that you really want, just do as I do: ask the burly men in your entourage to indulge you! I'm certain that one of them will happily oblige.

WARRIOR HUGS – Classification: Wrapping/A-Frame

I've included this martial-arts hug to show how hugging is used in the more aggressive and violent aspects of human nature, and not simply the warm and cuddly sorts.

From the beginning of time, clans and societies have waged war, fighting each other for dominance over one thing or another. Before the smart bomb, the tanks, the guns, the swords and the arrows, there was martial combat. Two combatants, usually men, would use their bodies, wits, and will to survive and bring either glory or dishonour to their clan.

Every martial art in existence finds its roots and inspiration here. Combining strength, agility, speed, flexibility, mental fortitude and strategy, Warrior Hugs are noble and powerful fighting techniques. They are used to overpower and subdue an opponent— especially common in the grappling arts of judo and jujitsu, as well as in sumo, Greco-Roman, freestyle and professional wrestling and some kickboxing styles such as Muay Thai, known as Thai boxing in North America.

In grappling, fighters use body-hugging techniques to keep close to and press up against one or more critical areas on an opponent's body in order to minimize the leverage of their actions, with the aim of throwing them down to the ground where they can be pinned and subdued.

Over the years, professional wrestlers have developed countless flashy holds with equally flamboyant names, many derived from judo or jujitsu, some invented by wrestlers themselves. The Scoop Slam, Sunset Flip, Gutwrench and Tilt-a-Whirl are just a few of the hugging moves used by the gladiators of this popular spectacle.

Thai boxing is a devastating martial art where the combatants use exclusively their hands, elbows, knees and feet to vanquish their opponent. An A-Frame type hug is used when a fighter wants to use his opponent's resistance to launch a powerful knee or shin strike.

Healing Hugs

When our hearts are touched by the tender hand of love, hope illuminates our path and helps us find the fortitude to face life with gratitude and courage. Human touch holds the potential for the nurturing and care of body, mind, spirit and heart. So whether you want to soothe your own suffering, join the loving beauty of your heart with that of another, or welcome the Divine Spirit into you with humility, these magical hugs are yours to cultivate.

Healing Hugs are the most precious jewels in this treasury, for they will bring a sparkle to your eye, a glow to your heart and a richness of spirit that will help make of life a worthy and meaningful adventure.

SELF-HUG – Classification: Wrapping

We all go through periods in our lives when we are feeling particularly vulnerable, emotional or out of touch with ourselves. Sometimes we ignore our needs, and forget the importance of caring, loving and respecting our body, mind, heart and spirit.

The turn of the millennium was a difficult time for me, as I was dragging too much of my past with me into a new era. A broken heart, a divided spirit, and a loss of faith in a kind and loving world—these were just part of the baggage that I had burdened myself with. I didn't know from one day to the next whether my life was beginning or ending. Still, I knew enough to understand that I had to live my experience one day at a time, one moment at a time, if I was to ever see the light of hope again. My past explorations in meditation and mindfulness had taught me that nothing lasts forever and tomorrow is always a different day, a new beginning with endless possibilities.

It was easy to know in my mind what I had to do, but to actually transform my knowledge into action was much more difficult. For two solitary years I wept for forgiveness, prayed for guidance, and searched for understanding. I sat in silence and waited for the hand of inspiration to come and lift me out of the abyss. My prayers were answered one day: the Spirit of life touched me, with my own hand, with my own embrace. It was while holding myself with tenderness

and love that I found solace, comfort, and the resolve to face my suffering and begin my journey of healing and redemption.

Now, when I feel disconnected with my inner self, disturbed, overly worried, or out of sorts, I simply take a quiet moment to hug myself. I begin by creating an environment of silence and tranquility. Then I seat myself comfortably on my meditation cushion and wrap my arms around myself. Closing my eyes, I observe my breath as it flows deeply and naturally through me. Eventually my body begins to gently sway.

I might sing or chant; I find that doing this brings an added sense of sacredness to the experience. There are times when a strong surge of emotion will well up inside me and I will begin to weep uncontrollably, or to giggle or become overly agitated. This used to worry me, but I don't concern myself with it anymore because I know that it's normal for emotions to emerge when I'm reconnecting with my heart centre. I just let the emotion flow through me and continue cradling myself. Within a few minutes the disturbances in my mind begin to calm, a sense of peace envelops me, and I am able to reconnect with my sense of being. What a joy it is to be home again. Home really is where the heart is: within ourselves.

After fifteen minutes or so, depending on time and need, I end the hug or continue with a period of meditation, reflection or prayer. This invites closeness with the Sacred within, and allows me to express gratitude for the comfort and guidance I have received.

CRADLING HUG — Classification: Wrapping

Physically, this is almost identical to the Patting Hug, but the similarity ends when we look at its intention. The intention invested in this hug is one of deep caring and tender compassion. Generally there is one person consoling and one being consoled, though it does happen that two people who need consoling will comfort each other, weeping and hugging together or in turn. Even when this is the case, there is almost always one who will be a pillar of strength for the other.

When comforting someone this way, I imagine myself cradling a tiny, fragile, precious child, which we all are when in a vulnerable state. If emotion wells up in them I'll hold them a little closer and even gently rub the nape of their neck or head with my hand. This is a very intimate, comforting gesture; it lets the consoled person know that they are safe in your care and that you are attentive to their distress. As a natural reflex, the person may bury their face into your shoulder and cry. This is wonderful, as the release of suppressed emotion can be very cathartic. I find that adding a gentle rocking or cradling motion to the embrace amplifies the comfort quotient. When you accompany this with tender, supportive words or even soft singing, the effect is very potent. This hug lasts for as long as it has to. I always let the receiver decide when it is enough. This is their time to heal, so I honour it with my undivided and unrushed attention.

If you are the one being consoled and you feel safe in the person's arms, then let yourself go; let yourself melt into the embrace, and allow your suffering to surface so that it can receive the comfort that's being offered. This hug is a healing gift from the heart, and

it is yours to cherish. Afterwards, take the time you need to acknowledge each other, and remember to express gratitude to one another.

A Note of Awareness:

When I wrote "supportive words," I meant just that. Telling a distressed person not to cry, or saying that life isn't that bad, or that everything will be just fine—these things are not supportive, they're critical. Besides, a person who's upset doesn't want to hear it, because in their present reality life is not fine. Saying these things is disrespectful. If their distress makes you uncomfortable, it's better to remain silent and strong then to give them invalidating platitudes. Caring silence can bring much comfort. If words seem necessary, then tell them you are there for them and they are safe in your arms. This is a selfless hug. Your sole focus is to support and comfort your partner in their time of distress. If you don't know what to say, trust that your hugging presence alone will suffice.

MINDFULNESS HUG – Classification: Wrapping

To be mindful is to be consciously aware of what you are experiencing from moment to moment. During the late 90s I spent part of my winters at Manzanita Village, a secluded meditation retreat center in southern California. Under the guidance of my friends and spiritual teachers, Caitriona and Michele, I learned to deepen my meditation practice, develop mindful awareness and become a kinder, gentler soul. It was there on the edges of the Anza

Borrego Desert that my spiritual practice took root and flourished, showing me a way to incorporate meditation and mindfulness into my daily life. There, I was introduced to a variety of meditation techniques: insight meditation, loving kindness meditation, working meditation, walking meditation and even hugging meditation, which was created by my teachers' teacher, Vietnamese Zen Master Thich Nhat Hanh.

The Mindfulness Hug is structured, formal and reverent. Keep in mind that it was created in precisely this way by a Buddhist monk, who was faced with the dilemma of expressing himself in a manner foreign to his culture in order to meet the needs of a more physically demonstrative American lay community. The following is a description of hugging meditation, or the Mindfulness Hug, as I remember it.

My hugging partner and I face each other with an attitude of respect and reverence. We each take a slow, deep breath, while placing our palms together in a prayer position, and then bow to each other. Bowing is a way to recognize a person's presence while acknowledging in your heart that the Divine sacredness in you honours the Divine sacredness in them. After the bow we step forward and embrace each other.

Now we come to the heart of the hug, which lasts for three slow, deep breaths. During the first breath I am mindful of my aliveness, my presence in this place, and my pleasure in simply being here now.

During the second breath I become mindful of my partner, of their presence in this place and of my pleasure in being here with them now. On the third and last breath, I become aware of the warmth, tenderness and beauty that sharing this moment with another human being has brought to me. I am filled with loving kindness for them. With this intention in my heart I slowly separate from my partner, step back and bow to them once again with appreciation and gratitude. That was how I, through mindfulness, learned to hug the moment.

This mindful approach to hugging brought a formal sacredness and a real sense of compassionate intimacy to an activity that I had always thought to be just a casual greeting. Looking back today, I can sincerely say that my experiences at Manzanita Village had a profound, life-changing impact on me. There on the edge of the desert, the seeds of loving kindness and mindful respect for other human beings and life itself where sown, so that years later the Hugger Busker could take root in my fertile heart, and mature and blossom into my life's joy. For this gift I am eternally grateful.

HEARTFELT HUG – Classification: Wrapping
(The Hugger Busker's Hug)

I am often asked what makes my hugs so special that people would come back again and again and even send their friends to hug me.

How would I describe my hugging technique? Well, it's a mix of several kinds of hugs in this section; a bit of self-hug, a bit of cradling hug, a bit of mindfulness hug and a bit of soul hug. But then, technique is not what makes for a heartfelt hug; loving intention does. The hugs that I offer are heartfelt, meaning that they are infused with unconditional love, kindness, care, reverence and joyful surrender to the glory of God within all of us.

Here is one way that recipients of the heartfelt hug have described the experience: "It was a very deep and moving experience. His hug was much more genuine then I expected and certainly more intimate. When we began hugging, I felt the strength of his hands on my back as he held me, and gently pulled my chest up against his. It was very comforting, even intimate. I felt him breathe deeply; it was slow and filling. This brought a calm over me and I could let myself go in his embrace. It was then that I felt this incredibly powerful energy exchange as my heart chakra fully opened and our hearts connected. We held each other for quite a long time. We both sighed as we tightened our embrace and then we both giggled. It was beautiful! Then he relaxed his hold and we slowly came apart. We looked at each other and smiled. Afterwards, I felt such a profound sense of peacefulness, joy and love, so much so that I felt compelled to reach out to others in my life in the same way."

This is not to say that everyone who hugs me will experience it in this way. It all depends on a person's receptivity and the depth of connection we feel. Though my desire to hug does not change, my ability to give of myself does since my energy level, my openness and my moods vary from day to day, and even from hug to hug. Hugging is an exchange of intention and energy, and though I may give a hug from the heart, that doesn't mean that my partner will necessarily receive it with their heart.

As of the writing of this book I have shared well over 45,000 hugs, and even so I endeavour to treat every hug as the first and last one that I will ever experience. This attitude helps me to feel a freshness and a sense of discovery with each and every hug, and that makes hugging a true adventure.

SOUL HUG – Classification: Formal

This rare jewel is a greeting of the spirit, one that is exchanged, among others, by some Tibetan monks. I've included it here because I feel that it's a profoundly intimate way of connecting with the core of another person's being. For me a soul hug is a spiritual hug.

In Formal form, the two monks stand facing each other as soul brothers, looking at one another with warmth and joyful recognition. Breathing deeply, they share a smile, and like in the Mindfulness Hug, they bow with reverence. Maintaining their awareness of their breath and of each other, they lean their heads forward until their foreheads touch gently at the spot between and just above the eyebrows. Buddhist traditions call this spot the third eye, the seat of enlightened awareness and understanding. With eyes closed, both continue to breathe deeply, staying aware of the other's intimate presence. After for several full breaths they separate, bow and go on their way. It is a beautiful and touching ritual to observe, but much more wonderful still to take part in.

Sharing a soul hug is always an enriching experience for me and since I began writing this book, I have indulged in it with more regularity, especially with my close friends. The experience brings an immediate sense of interconnectedness, inner peace and soul bonding that is unparalleled.

When trying this, don't forget the importance of your breath. Breath is the life-giving force that unites us with all living things, and makes us more conscious of being one with the Universe.

FORGIVENESS HUG – Classification: Formal

This is identical to the Soul Hug, but I've adapted it specifically for two individuals who need to heal their wounded hearts and come closer together in forgiveness and acceptance—a couple, a pair of friends, two siblings, a parent and child. It is also a good way for a couple to check in with each other and deepen their bond. I have experienced this hug on a number of occasions and it has really helped strengthen communication and understanding in my relationships.

When fear, anger, hurt or mistrust has driven a wedge between you and someone you love, it is often difficult to find reconciliation with out falling into the traps of blame, guilt and recrimination. Often we lack an environment in which each individual can express their suffering, their longings and their needs in a safe and respectful way. If both participants are willing, the Healing Heart Hug allows for deep listening, reconciliation and bonding. It creates a clean slate in which both people can hear each other, forgive each other and move forward.

The couple can take as much time as needed with this hug. I strongly suggest that you hold hands during this ritual. As with the Soul Hug, the two people must approach each other with an attitude of reverence, absolute respect and humility, while breathing slowly and deeply, looking into each other's eyes, and allowing for silence and calm to settle.

At this point, refrain from speaking. You will do that soon enough. When feelings of nervousness, apprehension, and discomfort arise, be compassionate with yourself and your partner; they will pass. After five breaths, touch your foreheads and close your eyes. Maintain your mindfulness of the present moment. After ten full breaths or so, one of you can begin to express what emerges from your heart, whether that is words of sadness, hurt, forgiveness, love, appreciation, or whatever else arises that needs to be said. When both of you have shared your truths, slowly separate your heads, open your eyes and reconnect with each other. Smile, cry, laugh, hug, cuddle... let your tenderness inspire you to maintain this renewed closeness through out the day.

A Note of Awareness:

It is important for the healing process that each speak in turn and about their own feelings, without bringing in blame or accusation. Strive to express yourself from the perspective of statements that start with "I feel," "I need" or "I am." Listen to what the other has to say, and try to really hear them.

GOD'S HUG – Classification: Wrapping

It is true that prayer, communion with the Divine, is a very personal matter, an interior journey that cannot really be shared with another. But it is possible to be prayerful together, to find togetherness in communion with the Spirit. In spiritual spaces people often pray or meditate next to one another, but to actually establish and maintain close physical contact during this ritual can be a very powerful form of spiritual and emotional bonding. You are not only opening your hearts to God individually, but you are also offering up the hopes, struggles and dreams of the two people to the sanctity of God's loving light.

Jade and I practice this hug regularly. Usually Jade will sit on her meditation cushion with her back straight and her legs crossed or bent open in front of her. I will then take my place on the same cushion, sitting snugly behind her. If you wish to try this, but sitting on a floor cushion is not suitable, you can sit one behind the other on the edge of a couch or chair. With my arms wrapped around her, I will place my hands on her heart chakra and she will place hers on top of mine. With eyes closed we bring our awareness to the breath until we are breathing in unison. We will sit in silence breathing deeply and evenly for at least 15 minutes. Breathing in unison usually happens naturally, but if it doesn't, don't worry about it.

Now is the fun part. Imagine that your whole being is filled with loving, healing white light flowing out from your heart into your partner and back into you again, like the ebb and flow of the ocean's tide. With each breath the flow gets stronger, until you are both enveloped in a brilliant cocoon of white light. Know and trust that you both are safe and can offer up your fears, your worries and your suffering to the healing power of this light. At this moment when enveloped with luminescence, I feel as if I am being embraced by the Divine presence of God, hence God's Hug.

Jade and I end most of our meditations by sending the intention of love, gratitude and healing to people who aren't present with us—family, friends, or anyone else who comes to mind. For example, when a particular person enters into my thoughts, it's because they are connected to me in that moment, and that connection allows my loving intention to touch and heal them. We close the meditation with a silent prayer of gratitude and then we gently separate and acknowledge each other's presence.

After any meditation, it's best not rush on to something else, but rather to let yourself steep in the reflective silence of your inner being. In fact this is the perfect time to serve up that mint tea that has been brewing and enjoy being in each other's company. Can life be any more beautiful than this?

Intimate Hugs

At every stage of a romantic relationship the physical expression of intimacy between the two individuals who care for and love each other is paramount to the development and strengthening of their emotional, psychological and spiritual bond. In courtship, the how, what, when and where of touch seems to be at the top of the agenda; then, as commitment brings stability to the relationship, the level of touching and physical intimacy tends to decrease, and if it's not deliberately maintained it can eventually become nonexistent. Relationship therapists are constantly exploring new techniques to help their clients get back in touch with themselves and with each other in both sexual and non-sexual ways. Non-sexualized touch such as hugging, cuddling, hand-holding, massaging and caressing play a major role in letting both partners know that they are appreciated, respected, desired and loved. Passionate sex is great, but in and of itself that's not enough to sustain intimacy.

Without other forms of intimate touching and shows of affection, the relationship will suffer in the long term. An intimate, loving hug can go a long way in helping a couple reconnect and stay connected in mind, body, heart and spirit.

FRONT-TO-BACK HUG – Classification: Wrapping

Whether you enjoy it while you appreciate a romantic view of a glorious sunset, sink into it for comfort while witnessing the scene of a tragedy, or simply glide into it while watching the dogs play in the yard, this hug finds its place as a way to share your appreciation or heartache when faced with life's unfolding. These moments, significant or otherwise, are the stuff that life, memories and relationships are made of.

Many times I have found myself at the ocean's edge holding my lover tightly against my chest, as we look out onto the unfolding of the day. It fills me with peaceful contentment to feel her holding my hands to her heart while breathing in my embrace and surrendering to our shared silence. This hug helps us to feel that together, we are looking towards an unknown yet complicit future.

The Front-to-Back Hug is a unifying and emotionally intimate hug that holds in its embrace the intentions of hope, comfort, reassurance and acceptance. For couples, it can inspire faith in the potential of the partnership and expresses a common desire to move forward in life, together, knowing that whatever is being witnessed will bring them closer and not further apart. For others, especially strangers, it can be an instinctive act of support and comfort offered to someone in emotional or psychological distress. A profound silence usually accompanies this hug; words need not be spoken when the intentions of the hugger are intuitively understood.

DANCING HUG – Classification: Formal

For hopeful lovers and long-time lovers of all ages, the beautiful ritual of courtship and love called the slow dance can be sublime... or stressful. From high school gymnasiums to classy ballrooms, from chintzy reception halls to swanky nightclubs, in community centres and candlelit living rooms, this dancing hug has cast its seductive spell on countless romantics. How many of us are here today because our parents' love blossomed in the hypnotic sway of this embrace? I most certainly am!

There are two distinct variations to the slow dance. The first is formal and physically distant, and the other close and passionate. The latter variation will be discussed in the Dirty Dancing Hug.

Though the setting plays a part in determining how intimate a dancing hug will get, in most cases the determining factor will be the personal rapport between the individuals themselves. First-time daters who are still uncertain as to the level of rapprochement they are willing to invest in their budding courtship tend to slow dance in a more formal and physically distant way. Long-term couples may also be less physical as they have become so accustomed to each other's presence that to be overly demonstrative in expressing affection or desire in public is either inappropriate or unnecessary. Though formal in nature, the Dancing Hug can be infused with desire, tenderness and loving affection. There is much more eye contact than for many other hugs; here, communication is more important then sensation.

DIRTY DANCING HUG — Classification: Wrapping

This is the sensual, sexual version of the dancing hug—perfect for the adventurous, exhibitionistic, over-stimulated or just head-over-heels-in-love romantic duo, who wants the world to witness the passion and desire that their love or lust ignites. These charming couples are oblivious to the outside world at this point, being so absorbed in the fulfillment of their own hearts and loins.

Together they drift across the dance floor to a rhythm only they can hear. With hearts beating in their chests, breath mingling, draped arms wrapped around each other's swaying bodies, and legs and thighs insistently nudging at their passions, the couple seems to merge into one, enveloped in their intimacy. Meandering hands touch and caress, ears are nibbled, necks are nuzzled, and endearments are whispered... it all comes together to lead our two lovers from the centre of the dance floor to an environment more suitable to, well... other kinds of dancing!

SMOOCHING HUG – Classification: Wrapping

A natural extension to the Dancing Hug, or at least the Dirty Dancing Hug, this libidinous embrace is the universal anthem of new lovers around the world. If they don't have a love nest of their own or they hope to avoid curious, prying eyes, Smooching Huggers tend to favour secluded corners, empty stairwells, parked cars and out-of-the-way places. This is not to say that some bolder types won't stand in the middle of a grocery store aisle necking fervently. When the mood strikes I personally enjoy indulging in such displays of affection. They're very liberating!

I chose to name this the Smooching Hug because it is different then simply kissing; it's a combination of hugging, kissing and sensual touching. Smooching is, at least in my interpretation, an unhurried, sensual exploration of one's partner, through hugging, touching and, of course, kissing. You can smooch in any position, though standing or leaning tends to be more popular. Smooching can go on for hours as you take a breather now and then or indulge in affectionate banter. This advanced courting ritual can allow couples to explore each other more intimately

with out committing to complete physical intimacy.
On the other hand it can also entice them to be even
more adventurous, turning their sensual embrace into
a passionate one. This is one of the most sexual and
lustful hugs in the Treasury!

TANTRIC HUG – Classification: Wrapping

Tantra is a path to spiritual enlightenment that focuses on enhancing and transforming masculine and feminine sexual energy into spiritual energy. Tantric techniques use the physical body and breath to help practitioners find more joy and ecstasy in their lives by teaching them to be present in the reality of their sensorial self. The Tantric Hug, my name for the practice, is the most intimate and sensual hug in the Treasury.

When exploring the spiritual nature of sexuality, Jade and I like to create an atmosphere that inspires sacred sensuality: candles, music, incense, flowers, meaningful objects or body adornments, sensual foods or drinks, and anything else that will stimulate our senses and our desire. Together we prepare our space, then ourselves. We will share an aromatic bath, wash and dry each other, and let our desire grow with each glance, with each touch, with each breath. Then when we enter our sacred space, our sensual sanctuary, our senses are tingling with aliveness.

The Tantric Hug is all about developing comfort, complicity, trust and a deep connection between both partners, so don't be shy to really look at your partner, to really touch their heart and soul with your eyes, your fingers and your lips. This is about being sensual rather then sexual. This is a time to be playful, worshipful and curious. Breath is paramount in Tantra; it's what will ground you and connect you to each other. Throughout the ritual, maintain awareness of your breath, breathing deeply and evenly into your lower belly. When you are both ripe with desire it is time to engage in the Tantric Hug. (Please note that I'm providing the heterosexual version here because that's what I have experienced, but same-sex couples can certainly bring sacredness into their lovemaking by creating their own variations of the Tantric Hug.)

The woman faces her partner and slowly lowers herself onto him until she is fully penetrated by him. Once comfortably seated, she wraps her legs around his waist, hooking her feet behind him. Both will wrap their arms around each other in an embrace. From here the journey begins. It is not a race to orgasm, nor is it denial of orgasm; the Tantric Hug is a moment-by-moment sensual exploration leading to Oneness. Let the breath guide your rhythms. Experience the journey; let the destination take you by surprise. Should orgasm be attained, share your pleasure fully by looking into your partner's eyes. This can be a very powerful moment for both of you. Trust that your breath, your awareness, your intuition, and your desire for a profound bonding experience will guide you.

Cuddles

The cuddle is the hug's lazy sibling. The hug is an active, focused act of intimacy and bonding; its intent is deliberate and specific to the experience itself, which rarely lasts more then a few minutes. The cuddle, on the other hand, is the optimum laid-back lounging experience; it's unhurried, relaxed and casual. Comfort is the key to a great cuddle, which can last for hours. There is no purpose to cuddling apart from basking in someone's comfortable embrace while being involved in an activity other then the embrace itself. Intimate conversation, watching television, reading a good book, waking up or napping are but several examples of moments when cuddling may be the hug of choice. This is not to say that a cuddle is pointless! Not at all. Cuddling is a wonderful way to spend precious time together!

CASUAL CUDDLE

I had just finished writing the introduction to this section when Jade arrived home with our favourite take-out dish: General Tao chicken and mixed veggies with tofu in black bean sauce. While she made a pot of Japanese green tea, I grabbed a couple of pillows and threw them on the couch. With our bowls and chopsticks in hand, we lay back and snuggled together on the couch to share a simple meal, tea, a

DVD and each other's company. We were ready for a night of comfortable togetherness at the movies. We don't always watch movies when we cuddle; we both lead very busy lives and often the evening is the only quality time that we get to spend with each other. So when we cuddle on the couch or in the hammock, we reconnect and share the adventures of our day. For us this simple form of intimacy creates deeper bonding than being sexually intimate. Of course cuddling has been known to lead frisky folks to unrestrained naughtiness, but that's another book altogether. Just as individuals need quiet time for themselves, couples need quiet time together to connect in a non-sexualized way, especially if they are parents.

You can cuddle with your pets, your kids, your friends and your whole family if the mood strikes. Family cuddles are a great way to build and maintain family spirit and unity, where trust, support, playfulness and unconditional love can be expressed. This can also be a good way to introduce the young ones to these wonderful rituals of togetherness, so that they may in turn adopt them and use them in their own lives. If we want our children to grow up being comfortable with themselves and having the ability to express their intimate needs in a healthy way, then it is important to teach them that it's beautiful and natural to give and receive affection.

Cuddling can become a cherished ritual in the life of a couple or a family if they take the time to truly share being with each other. With monster TVs, video games and other entertaining distractions vying for our attention, cuddling time can easily end up being passed in solitary togetherness rather then in shared intimacy. Though together physically, people may remain in their own world, distracted and disconnected from each other. Try to remember that, in spite of the distractions, you are sharing this time with a loved one. No matter where you do it, cuddling is an optimal environment for communication and intimacy to flourish... just make sure you nourish it a little bit along the way.

COCOONING

At certain times, we need to take a pause from the rigours of the outside world and reacquaint ourselves with the world within. Whether we're feeling fear, distress, unease or simply a need for solitude, cocooning provides the comforting isolation reminiscent of the warm and safe confines of the womb. Though it is an act of self-love in the spirit of self-hugging, it is also an act of self-preservation.

A number of breath-focused therapies use cocooning as a technique to encourage healing and transformation. There are no arms enveloping you, only a big, fluffy comforter or blanket wrapped tightly around you. There you lie in the dark coziness of solitude, where every sensation within becomes your reality, where every emotion can be revealed and suffering healed. Your cocoon is a quiet, private place where you can escape from the struggles of life,

where you can reflect and face your truth. It's a safe space to be entirely with yourself, where you can shed the attachments that bind your beauty and, like a butterfly, be reborn into life with renewed hope and fortitude.

A Note of Caution:

If you are at all claustrophobic or have breathing problems, you might want to leave your face or head exposed to facilitate breathing.

SPOONING

When you take two spoons and place one into the other they fit snugly together. So it's not surprising that this cuddle may be the perfect fit for a sleeping or napping couple. The warmth, the satisfaction, the coziness and the peacefulness that this cuddle brings are reminiscent of being in the womb, only *à deux*. No wonder twins often have such a powerful bond! Spooning is a way to develop this kind of symbiotic bond between two intimates. Why this is called spooning and not forking is beyond me—don't two forks fit together well, too? Anyway, a perfect fit is a perfect fit no matter the form!

Like two spoons, both partners snuggle close one behind the other, finding the perfect position to snooze and dream. Spooning is also a popular sexual position as it is very sensual and intimate, allowing for close full-body contact but leaving the hands free to touch and stimulate. It's also a very comfortable position for intercourse during pregnancy.

MORNING CUDDLE

Jade insisted that I add this most Divine jewel to my collection as it has inspired her to bring in the newness of each day with grace and confidence.

Every morning, as the day finds its way into our waking hearts, we roll towards each other and entwine our limbs tightly together to bring our bodies into a slumbering embrace. During those precious minutes, we can put off the cares of the coming day for just a while longer and rejoice in the cares of the heart.

I asked Jade to write down what our morning ritual meant to her. Here are her words: "Welcoming this day in love, comfort and tenderness reassures me; I know that I am not alone on my journey, and that no matter what the day brings I feel supported and appreciated by my partner's presence and love."

As for me, I feel that our morning cuddles have deepened our level of intimacy and complicity. Our morning affection has certainly played an important part in helping us face the few difficult moments in our relationship with optimism and respect. Our ritual cuddling, nurtured with tender caresses and endearing words, has become such an important aspect of our bonding that when we pass up a morning cuddle we spend the day missing it.

There are times when in spite of our best intentions, one of us has gone to sleep feeling upset. This cuddle has helped us both find forgiveness and renewed faith in our partnership and our desire to

remain together. It doesn't take much to maintain
harmony and loving in a relationship: a touch of
appreciation, a word of support, an act of caring and
an attitude of respect. Bringing each of these elements
into our relationship every single day has helped
deepen the roots of our union so that it can continue
to grow and blossom, season after season.

BUBBLY CUDDLE

I don't know about you, but I love taking baths. It could be because I don't have a shower and my bath is an old, deep cast-iron antique that fits two people just perfectly. No matter the reason, I am happy soaking away my cares, covered in bubbles with my rubber ducks and lotus flowers floating about as I read a good book or cuddle my beloved. When I lived in Thailand, a local girl introduced me to the pleasures of mutual bathing at the edge of a small stream surrounded by forested mountains, rice paddies and a golden setting sun. From that moment I was hooked, and the sensual beauty and romantic essence of shared bathing and washing have since become a treasured part of my cleansing rituals.

A steamy shower for two can be stimulating and tantalizingly fun; showering is also an option if you lack a suitable bath, and it can be a great way to energize your day. Still, there is nothing like a hot, aromatic, bubbly soak, cuddle and scrub to ease the tensions of the day and raise your passions for erotic play. Whether you love to bathe or prefer to shower, the truth is that sharing either one will definitely spice up your romance.

A romantic Bubbly Cuddle requires a few essentials: a bath tub suitable for the occasion, candles, aromatic oils, bath gel (for the bubbles), a big bath sponge, good ambient music, a handful of rose petals thrown in for good measure (which you can get at any florist), a pot of chai tea on the side, a book of erotic poetry and a few large fluffy towels for the after-cuddle.

Cuddling Parties

A strange, new breed of socializing has cropped up in numerous cities across North America. It's becoming all the rage to hold parties where people meet to cuddle! I see this as the trend of the present and the wave of the future. Cuddling parties are an affectionate social event of choice for friends, couples and strangers alike who want to share playful, non-sexual physical intimacy and communication with others in a safe, trusting and non-judgmental environment. On the menu: unconditional affection, tender touching, nurturing care, and authentic communication.

Participants in cuddling get-togethers will meet at a pre-designated location, change into their niftiest pyjamas, grab their favourite stuffed animal or pillow and plop their sweet cuddly selves down on one of many cozy, comfy spaces available. You might be invited to cuddle with one other person or with a group, or you might do the inviting. Then again, you may just want to go solo for a bit. People will cuddle, touch, kiss, talk, listen, and just be present in the experience of intimate non-sexual togetherness. No fondling, inappropriate touching, rubbing or petting is allowed, nor are intoxicants or mind-altering substances. There might even be a PM (party monitor) or two to watch over the sanctity of the space and to enforce the rules to ensure a safe and happy cuddling experience for all!

Multi-Person Hugs

We are not islands isolated in the vastness of an ocean, succumbing in solitude to the ever-changing tide of life. Rather, we are the droplets that make up that ocean's waves, insignificant apart yet yielding powerful transformative energy when united. It is the same with a couple, a family, a group, a team, a community. It is when we come together in life's flow that trust, understanding, respect, and the spirit of unconditional love can grow.

A hug is certainly not the exclusive domain of twosomes. In fact the more people that add themselves to a hug, the more energizing and fun it can become. There is no limit to how many people can hug. To date the official record for the largest group hug tells us that it brought together 5,117 participants. An amazing feat of togetherness! Organized hugging events, such as Rainbow Gatherings and day-long hugging festivals, take place around the world regularly, attracting hundreds and sometimes thousands of people from every spectrum of society. So whether there are three of you or five thousand, stretch out those arms, wrap your heart around the tender sweetness of humanity and let the celebration begin!

TRIANGLE HUG

Hugging a couple is one of my favourite ways to hug. It's sublime to bask in the light of loving affection that the lovers have for each other! Many newlyweds have shared a hug with me, and every time, I feel honoured to be a part of their vibrant intimacy. When a couple receives love and affection as a unit rather then as individuals, this acknowledges their commitment and affirms the love they have for one another.

When I hug a couple I find myself naturally embracing them as one rather then as two separate individuals. I intend no disrespect to the individuals themselves; it's simply that the complicit intimacy of their connection bonds them as one, and that's how they instinctively approach the embrace. So I gather them in my arms and together we honour their union.

Couples are often surprised at how wonderful

this makes them feel afterwards. It brings me much satisfaction to watch them walk away hand-in-hand, or holding each other close when they may not have been touching before the hug.

With non-couple triangles, there are three individual energies and levels of intimacy to contend with rather then two. Girlfriends might share secrets like this, siblings might give support, team-mates might confer, strangers might find comfort, and children might playfully plot mischief.

Family Hug

There is something wonderfully endearing about seeing the members of a family hold each other in a strong, loving embrace. It can be difficult to sustain supportive and loving family unity, but it is possible if you take the time to be aware of and present with each other. Little moments like shared laughter, a tender touch, an appreciative smile or a playful exchange can bond a family together. Time is the greatest gift that a parent can give their child, as it makes them feel wanted, appreciated and worthy of attention and love. When family members take the time to celebrate and honour each other with genuine love, respect and appreciation, the effect reverberates for generations to come. A hugging family is a loving one! A laughing family is a joyful one! How better to concretize that bond than through a family hug?

When you come together in a close hug, remember to pick up the little ones or bend down to accommodate the shorter members of your family. Having your face squished into someone's belly in the spirit of togetherness is not fun. As for the shy, stubborn ones who squirm, giggle and try to pull away, or who obstinately refuse to join in, I suggest playfully surrounding them with laughter and tenderness. In most cases they will melt grudgingly but gratefully into the familial embrace, but if not, then leave them be and continue with your fun—they will eventually miss the amusement and join in.

Respecting others' limits is always paramount, but there are times we must not be afraid to show loving

compassion by pushing those limits when we know that it will bring someone the love and comfort that they clearly need.

GROUP HUG

When three or more people gather together to form an impenetrable mass of bodies, a group hug is born. Whether it's spontaneous and disorganized or focused and purposeful, this hug can be used to celebrate events such as birthdays, graduations, and victories, or to unite individuals who share a common experience or purpose in a supportive and loving way. The dynamics of the two vary slightly in approach and intention.

The first method is when many people spontaneously assemble into one large, disorganized mass of embracing arms and compressed bodies. It is liberating, fun and wonderfully energizing for all involved. Its intention is to amuse and celebrate, as well as promote team spirit and camaraderie. When forming this mass hug, the growing crush of bodies places a great deal of physical pressure on those at the centre, so make sure to compensate for it as best you can.

The second variation is slightly more orderly and deliberate, and the intention of those involved is consciously heartfelt and loving. The hug is layered where the two or three people at core of the hug hold each other in an embrace, they in turn are surrounded by others who hold them from behind in a heartfelt embrace, and on it goes, layer upon layer of happy humans hugging and loving.

A Note of Caution:

If you are uncomfortable or prone to panic when in small, tight spaces, then the centre of a group hug is not the place to be, as the crush of bodies can be very restrictive.

HUDDLE HUG

The Huddle Hug is a distinct kind of group hug. The difference lies in that there is no one in the centre; like a doughnut, it is empty in the middle. Having formed a tightly knit circle by holding shoulders or locking arms, the participants lean towards the centre slightly. This way the huddlers can see each other and communicate, sing, chant, pray or commune in the manner of their choice.

The Huddle is a formation integral to the playing of rugby and North American football. In rugby it is called a scrum. Players from each team form a tight huddle, the ball is dropped into it and the players

fight over who will get possession. In football the huddle is used at the beginning of each play, when the quarterback calls the play to his offensive line.

As for ordinary citizens who want to connect with their fellow beings in a more deliberate, formal and even ritualized way, the open formation of the huddle is a better option than the potentially claustrophobic nature of the Group Hug. There is also a sense of community in this hug that is absent in the Group Hug. The circular formation of this hug raises power within it; all participants are equal, surrounding the emptiness within, which is protected, sacred space. The circle is also associated with the idea of Oneness, wholeness and interconnectedness, which is the essence of hugging.

TEAM HUGS

It is through the celebratory rituals of sports teams that we can witness the greatest variety of group hugs, and the most dynamic ones. Athletes in the throes of victory bring a surge of adrenaline, power and excitement to the group hug that is infectious in its exuberance, enticing even people watching on television to join in the fun. Team hugs express camaraderie and jubilation rather then tenderness and intimacy. As the game-ending whistle blows, with a sudden burst of ecstatic abandon, everyone involved in winning the game pours out onto the playing area to celebrate victory. What evolves from this outpouring is one or several of the following variations.

The Collision – Players, and sometimes fans, run onto the field and collide with each other, creating a massive group hug-fest. People have been known to bang into each other with such enthusiasm that some are knocked down like bowling pins. On occasion, part of the group is pushed off balance and crumples to the ground, creating an unintentional Pile-Up.

The Pile-Up – Players throw themselves on top of each other until they are all in one big pile.

The Herd – Similar to a collision, but the group is smaller and on the move. Usually when the scorer is running around in celebration, the other players will catch up and hug him on the run, ending up with a group of huggers moving together through the field. Like a herd of bison moving in unison at top speed, the Herd Hug is quite a spectacle.

The Hug and Run – The winning player is again running off the field while individual players catch up to her and hug her briefly as she is on the run.

The Convergence – The whole team converges onto the field, creating a tight hug. The hug itself is focused on celebrating one particular individual more than the group as a whole, such as the star player or coach, who will be at the centre of this hug. They may eventually be hoisted up on shoulders and carried about in celebration.

Cinnamon Roll Hug

A human cinnamon roll is what this hug feels like: sweet, spicy and oh-so-warm and tender. It was taught to me by a group of college students one day, who claimed that it was a ritual greeting amongst freshmen on their campus. I have an adventurous spirit and am not one to turn down a group hug no matter how whimsical it sounds, so I welcomed their instruction.

They had me stand in at the centre of the public square and they formed a line beside me. Everyone held hands with the people on either side of them. Being at the end of the line, I stood on my spot while the person at the head of the line began to run circles around me, leading the others in the line to wrap

themselves around me until a tight hug formed with me in the middle, creating a human cinnamon roll. Once the line was completely wrapped up, everyone threw their arms up and shouted cheerfully!

It was a ton of fun that left everyone involved energized and beaming. Isn't the point of enjoying the company of others to actively engage in joy through the pursuit of joyful activities, joyful expressions, and joyful being? Being joyful does not come easily to most of us; we have to work at it, to break through the grimness that inhabits us, the staid habits that hold us in our imagined proper place. But the only true proper place is a place where the heart is free to share its joyful song with other like-hearted souls.

HUG-INS

Hug-Ins are events where hundreds of people from all walks of life gather, usually in forested areas, with one purpose: to share as much love, tenderness and non-sexualized affection as possible in the hours, days, or even weeks that they are together. These gigantic events are infused with a spirit reminiscent of the love-ins of the Sixties; hugs, cuddles and huddles of every colour and hue abound.

The oldest and best known of these happenings are the Rainbow Gatherings, which take place several times a year at locations around the globe. These gatherings have even spawned tribes or families, each representative of their region or country. Like the travelling troubadours of the past, these cheerful companions wander the globe promoting a utopian

approach to living where respect, generosity, love and community spirit are the founding principles.

I have never attended a gathering of this kind, but I did once have a rapturous encounter with members of the French Rainbow Family. I remember it being a dull, grey afternoon—a slow day for hugging until twenty youthful, smiling, middle-aged Europeans dressed in vibrant earthy colours slowly congregated in the square before me, taking in the stillness of my offering. Then, as if by symbiosis, they formed a winding queue before me, each in turn sharing with me a very sincere heart-warming hug. What surprised me was that none of the hugs were hurried; each lasted as long as it needed to, some for several minutes.

Most people, when they hug me, keep it short and formal. But these were some of the most authentic

and loving hugs I have ever given and received. It was obvious that these beautiful human beings not only gave from the heart but lived from the heart. When I finally finished hugging the last one, they all gathered around me for a momentous group hug that just went on and on. It ended with them dancing around me, chanting in French, "Martin, le Roi des Câlins!" or "Martin, the King of Hugs!" I laughed in sheer delight and when I looked up, even the sky in all its greyness shone brightly.

Discordant Hugs

Discordant: not being in accord, conflicting, not harmonious.

The hugs described in this section are not gems, as they are not heartfelt, loving and fun; nor do they seem to have any redeeming values, apart from being a living testament to how badly some people deal with physical affection, and so are worthy of mention. These hugs are not to be emulated, unless you want to quickly become unpopular with your huggable friends. Rather, you might keep them as reminders of what might be expected when hugging complete strangers. You see, even hugging can be strange and disagreeable! We are human, and as such we develop all kinds of odd and even disturbing eccentricities to quiet our fears and satisfy our needs. Just look at me—I stand in public places and offer free hugs to complete strangers for a living! Some people find that to be very bizarre behaviour for a grown man. If only they knew the half of it.

The following experiences have disturbed, annoyed and even angered me. Though I promote non-judgment, compassion and unconditional love, I find it very difficult sometimes to deal with the baggage some people carry, no matter what their story. Over time I have become more tolerant, understanding and even appreciative of the disturbing side of human nature, but I am still far from being a completely selfless, loving, and compassionate enlightened being.

MACHO HUG – Classification: Wrapping

After having my spine pummelled and driven through my chest on a number of occasions by this sort of forceful greeting, I decided that it had earned the title of the most macho hug of them all. It's physically identical to the patting hug in every respect, except that it features an unhealthy dose of testosterone and ego. This hug is a bruising testament to how the experience of physical intimacy with another man can turn an insecure male into a hugging brute.

This hug is generally practiced by young men in their late teens and early twenties. The men who do it are somewhat uncomfortable with the physical intimacy of embracing another man, but they want to hug anyway. They will respond to my embrace by wrapping their arms around me firmly, but then instead of patting me gently on the back they will begin slapping their hand on my back steadily, until it becomes pounding. The longer the hug last the harder they pound. I assume that this shows their manliness to the watching world, or maybe it just represses the sensitivity that is trying to emerge. Whatever the case, I always stop this hug short for concern of actually being hurt.

Afterwards I usually try to speak with the individual to make him aware that his actions caused discomfort and hurt. I often offer to hug them again if they will allow themselves to be less aggressive and more receptive to the intimacy that the hug creates. Some men have accepted, and found that being gentle did not make them less masculine; in fact it made them feel stronger and more in control. The ones that refused would walk away, not understanding what my problem was. Either way I respected myself and in the process gave someone the opportunity to discover hugging in a different way.

CORPSE HUG — Classification: Formal

Imagine someone so unenthused by the idea of getting a hug that they just stand there like an empty shell or a listless corpse while you embrace them in a deep-felt way. It makes me want to shake them silly to wake them from their vegetative existence. You probably won't have to hug someone like this, but in my practice everyone is welcome and deserving; as long as they make their way into my waiting arms a tender embrace is theirs for the taking.

A lively woman with whom I had just shared a very endearing hug was trying to convince her young son and husband to get a hug from me. The boy came willingly and left with a happy smile. The husband was another story. He had the most morose and dejected look I had ever seen; unhappiness seemed to exude from his every pore. He did not come easily, but he came nonetheless at his wife's insistence. He trudged up and stopped before me. I thought that he was going to open his arms at least, but no. He simply stood there, arms dangling limply by his sides, staring at me with sad eyes. If anyone needed a hug, this man did. As I usually do, I asked him if I could offer him a hug, because I won't impose a hug on anyone. He did not answer. Instead he gave a slight grudging nod; I could almost hear him thinking, "Let's get it over with." So I took him in my arms and held him with as much loving comfort as I had in me. There was absolutely no response from him. Apart from his breathing he felt absent in my embrace. It was difficult to maintain the hug because my energy seemed to pass right through him. His depressed state was depleting my energy and his negative energy was making me feel queasy, so I ended the hug and sent him off with a few kind and supportive words.

I felt happy because I thought I had done something good for this sad man, but as he walked away he threw up his hand and gave me the finger. The joy that I was basking in suddenly vaporized. My face must have betrayed what I felt because the people watching became deathly silent, the man's wife included. I silently returned to my stillness as he approached her with a defiant smirk on his face. She gave him a resounding slap that stunned us all, and she then proceeded to loudly berate him. Taking the boy by the hand, she raged off, leaving the poor man standing in the middle of the crowded square with a hapless, miserable look on his face.

We all have our story, and everything we think, say or do affects its unfolding. Whether we improve our lot or worsen it, the choice is always ours to make.

HUG-ME-NOT HUG – Classification: Formal

Some people feel that it is impolite to refuse a hug, even though they would rather not be hugged or even touched. You can recognize a Hug-Me-Not Hugger by the way their whole body tenses the moment you embrace them. Their shoulders rise up, their arms and hands remain protectively close to their body, and they stop breathing for the duration of the embrace. The slightly less reluctant may actually gingerly pat the other person's upper back once or twice before prying themselves away with a polite smile. The odd thing is that this kind of hugger will never actually say no to being hugged or physically pull away from physical contact, even though their body screams, "Don't touch me!"

Every once in a while my sister, Annik, becomes a Hug-Me-Not Hugger. When she has her sullen, grin-and-bear-it look, I can tell that she is feeling emotional but is struggling to keep it in. She really needs a hug—I know it and she knows it—but she won't allow herself to get one. When I approach her, she will refuse, pulling her arms up defensively and sometimes even trying to push me off. But if I persist with humour and tenderness and then embrace her, she will melt gratefully and tearfully into my arms, content that I cared enough to reach beyond her façade of invulnerability and touch her aching heart. I love my sister deeply and am not afraid to show her, even if she is at times stubborn about accepting it.

In the end Annik always welcomes my hug after her initial resistance... but many others don't.

At first, I took offence when someone showed this kind of impassioned resistance. I would think, "Why the hell do they bother coming to me in the first place if they can't stand being hugged?" In time I realized that if I am to be a truly loving and considerate hugger, I must not impose my way of hugging on someone, but rather hug them in a way that they are capable of receiving.

My sister taught me that although I must respect people's limits, I should not be afraid to gently push those limits if it will bring the them the love and comfort that they most need. I always make it a point of thanking someone after sharing a hug with them, even if they gave nothing but their passive presence in return. By acknowledging to myself their innate goodness, their God nature, I find it much easier to accept the person I am hugging as they really they are, warts and all.

SUMO HUG – Classification: Wrapping

Entertaining for the viewing public, but not fun for me, this hug is the most disconcerting form of hugging that I have ever encountered. Imagine if you will, hugging a failed sumo wrestler who's experiencing flashbacks of his worst bouts in the ring. It is an awkward and disorienting experience that I would not recommend to any hugger.

The young, virile, insecure male who initiates this hug can easily come across as aggressive and even combative if you don't recognize his underlying desire to show affection. Very much like with the Macho Hug, the young man's intentions are not truly aggressive but rather an outward overreaction to feelings of insecurity and vulnerability brought on by the awkwardness of being physically affectionate with another man. He tries to re-establish control of the situation physically in order to counteract his rising feelings of discomfort.

This awkward two-step usually starts after the hug has begun. All is good until about the five-second mark, when the hug becomes a little more intimate then a casual pat on the back. This is when my hugger turns wrestler. He will suddenly tense up, tighten his grip on me and begin to physically twist, turn, lift and drag me about, as if I were a wilfully defiant opponent—which by that point I am quickly becoming. If this hug were not so disconcerting it would be quite funny. I don't like to be manhandled, so at this stage I will end the hug. As I firmly pry myself out of his agitated grip I inform him, in a polite but uncompromising tone, that hugging is not a combative affair, but one that is shared with someone, not imposed on them.

Hugging requires a caring approach, so if he is willing to give it another try I will show him that tenderness shared between two men is something to be enjoyed. As with the Macho Huggers, some accept and some don't. Whatever the outcome, I have left the door open for them to discover that hugging can be a bonding experience rather then a threatening one.

Variant Hugs

Hugging, like any art form, invites everyone to become an artist and express their own creativity. I encourage you to be creative, have fun, and bring your own original touch to hugging by freely interpreting, exploring, and adapting your hugs to suit your tastes and needs. Each situation calls for a unique approach. It is important to remain receptive and adaptable if you are going to make hugging a meaningful feature of your communication skills. Some of the following hugs deviate greatly from the standard body-to-body embrace, but with the right intention they remain true to the spirit of togetherness and loving kindness.

POWER HUG – Classification: Formal

As the Hugger Busker, I make it quite obvious to everyone that I give free hugs. My chalkboards clearly state my intention and my actions speak for themselves. Yet every day, someone will walk up and offer me their hand to shake. Maybe it's to test the seriousness of my convictions, or maybe they think they're funny, or maybe they are not the hugging type but want to show appreciation for what I do. Whatever the case, I refuse the offer and invite them instead to share a heartfelt hug. Some accept; others stubbornly insist that I shake their hand. This creates a dilemma that I have had to face with regularity, until I decided to offer the Power Hug, otherwise known as the President's Handshake.

I had heard that rich and powerful men did not shake hands with everyone they greeted equally. If you've ever observed, for example, how the President of the United States shakes hands with someone, from that simple gesture you can deduce that individual's importance to him. It always begins with a smooth, firm handshake. The difference lies in where the President places his left hand—directly on top of the hand being shaken, or gripping the forearm of that same hand, or patting the upper arm, or even placing his hand on top of the shoulder. The higher the President places

his left hand, the more personal his relationship is with the person, or the more importance the other has for him. This handshake makes the receiver feel appreciated and favoured in the presence of power.

To me this gesture felt like the perfect way to share solicitude with someone who insisted on a simple handshake. I call this a Power Hug because firstly, it empowered me to include those who, for their own reasons, felt unable to share a hug, yet still desired to connect with me. And secondly, it empowered them to know that their form of intimacy was as appreciated as a hug. Surprisingly, some of the men to whom I have given a Power Hug have returned at a later date to take me up on my original offer of a real hug. I had shown them respect by hugging them on their terms, and now they were returning the gesture.

PINKIE HUG

What happens when you find yourself in a situation where you need the comforting touch of a partner who is right next to you, but hugging them would be inappropriate given the context or company?

The Pinkie Hug came to me by way of the couple who designed the layout for this book. Richard and Samantha are two very huggable people. They told me that on many occasions, when at a business meeting or family dinner, if the urge to hug came to one of them, they would surreptitiously slip their hand under the table, grab the other's pinkie finger with their own, and squeeze it several times. This subtle, discreet gesture made it possible for them to physically connect in a way that just sharing a knowing glance would not have done. I thought that this hug was unique to Richard and Sam, but while talking to my friend Marc and his girlfriend I discovered that they and several other couples they know also use the Pinkie Hug regularly, as gesture of complicity.

Simple touch like this allows us to find affirmation in our daily lives; it reminds us that we are not alone, that there is someone out there with whom we can share a happy secret, whether they are family, friend or lover.

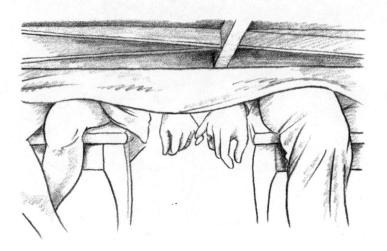

BOUNCING HUG – Classification: Wrapping

Playful, amusing and wonderfully endearing, though at times uncomfortable, this hug brings joyful delight to any child who is adventurous enough to go for a ride on the first robust leg that they find.

What family gathering, birthday celebration or holiday event has not had its share of equestrian games, especially when the favourite uncle or family friend comes to visit? Without fail, every three-year-old in the house wants to be the first to hop on his leg and go for a bouncy ride. Even Dad gets stuck with this sporting exercise every once in a while. It's not

that the adults mind the child's squeals of delight as they bounce about… it's only when the child won't let go, and insists on being dragged around like a dead weight, that things get awkward for parents and guests alike. The willing guest will usually grin and bear it with amusement as he walks about, or rather hobbles, as if one leg were shackled with iron ball and chain. It's a funny sight indeed and delightfully amusing… at least for the child!

TREE HUG – Classification: Wrapping

For a long time I never understood the point of hugging a tree. Why people practiced this strange ritual was beyond me. Did the tree feel any better after someone loved it, touched it and caressed it, or was it just a nifty slogan created by radical environmentalists to wake up the masses to the issue of deforestation? I remained in ignorance until I found myself in the presence of a 300-year-old oak as wide as two cars, somewhere along the Southern California section of the Pacific Crest Trail.

Drawn by the powerful majesty of this life-giving entity, I approached with awe and wonderment. What history was held in the memory of its being? What adventures had transpired around, above and beneath its branches? I stepped gingerly between the aged oak's tangled roots, and began exploring the gnarled surface with my fingertips until my arms had stretched out over its enormous girth. With my feet firmly planted in the rooted earth and my body pressed up snugly against the trunk, I closed my eyes, relaxed my grip and abandoned myself to the magnificent perfection of this life form. The mighty oak's vibrations spoke straight to the essence of my being, and its vitalizing breath coursed through my veins and rejuvenated my heart with the incessant rhythms of life. I felt my feet connect with its roots, my body with its trunk, my heart with its sap, its branches, its leaves, its fruit... I felt its energy mingle with mine... and then silence washed over and through me. I hugged that tree for an eternity of minutes. Then, slowly, as if waking from an ancient dream, I opened my eyes to the aliveness of the world around me. Serenity, vigour and acceptance had engulfed me. I sat under that tree for hours, unable to part from its presence. When I finally did resume my journey I departed with joyful sadness—the kind that one feels when leaving a cherished friend for a long period of time. The joy comes from knowing that their comforting presence rests deep within your heart, and the sadness remains because the memory of them will never compare with their actual presence.

Now, whenever I come across a tree that speaks to me or draws me to it, I hug it. As I do with people, I ask permission to hug before I do so. A tree has so many powerful qualities: the strength of its trunk, the flexibility of its branches, the grounding of its roots, the purifying nature of its leaves...While hugging I

let myself be intuitively guided by whatever quality I most need at that particular time and ask the tree to infuse me with it. I end every tree hug by expressing gratitude, recognition and respect for all that it provides: our life-sustaining air, protection from the elements, the structure of our homes, fuel to keep us warm and even the paper on which these words are printed.

AIR HUG – Classification: Wrapping

Recently I heard about a national air guitar competition, and I thought, why not Air Hugging? If you can blow a kiss across a room, you can hug from a distance too! Blowing a kiss is a romantic gesture, whereas Air Hugging can show sentiments where romance is not present. It sounds like a silly concept, but it can be very useful in certain situations. For this hug to have any redeeming value you must be separated from the object of your attention by a barrier or void of some sort, making them clearly visible but unreachable in any physical way. If you find yourselves on opposite sides of the subway tracks, a glass partition, a large crowd, or even a satellite broadcast, these might be ideal situations where an Air Hug is your saving grace.

There are two ways to do this. You can simply hug yourself while looking at your distant partner, and then send the hug their way as you would when blowing a kiss. Or you can actually send loving energy to them while doing it. To do this, place your hands at your heart centre. Take a slow, deep breath, focusing your attention on your partner, and then imagining that your arms are gigantic wings of loving light. Open them out to surround the object of your attention

with this light and draw them towards your heart. Wrap your arms around yourself, close your eyes for a brief moment, and then open your arms out from the heart to project the hug over to them. If you make your intention a truly loving one, they will feel it when they receive your hug, and wrap themselves in its symbolic embrace.

E-HUGS

Too far away to share a real hug with someone? Don't fret—now you can get online and send a cyber-hug! The Internet, via e-mail, chat rooms and instant messaging, is a fast and easy way to communicate with family, friends and strangers alike around the world. But not everyone is a skilled writer with the ability to clearly express their emotions with the written word. So for most of us, the spontaneity of expression and meaning is lost or even misinterpreted because you can't be seen or heard, only read.

Emoticons were developed to deal with this issue. They are an Internet chat shorthand that has evolved over the years from a few keystroke symbols expressing basic emotions (such as happy, sad, laughing or angry) into a language with hundreds of expressions and meanings. Most of us only need to know a dozen or so basic symbols for general chatting. Besides, nowadays most instant messenger programs have their own emoticon and "smiley" libraries available in the users' chat window. With a few keystrokes you can hug your friends around the world!

The four emoticons below are used in chat rooms, on message boards and in e-mail communication, each character string representing a type of hug.

Wanting to hug: [ ]

Sending a hug: []

Hugs and kisses: (()):**

Lots of hugs: ((((add person's name here))))

Icons and animated emoticons are becoming very popular in instant messenger programs as well. Typing the string >:D< in Yahoo, for example, will create an animated hug of an open-armed smiley hugging, while in MSN the strings (}) or ({) will create a static icon showing a head with two arms stretched straight out facing either right or left. Explore the keystrokes of the instant messenger program you use to see if you can create free hug icons, or if you want a greater variety, you can buy some really nifty animated ones from several online sites. Enjoy!

- 5 -

MEDITATIONS

Throughout this book I have shared with you my experiences with mindfulness, loving kindness and living from the heart. Here I offer you a few simple techniques that have helped me along my journey towards hugging life. I invite you to put aside a few minutes of your day to discover what a few deep breaths, some moments of silence, and warm smile can bring to your day.

These meditations can be done anywhere and at any time. It may be good to put aside at least 20 minutes during which you will be undisturbed. Loosen any restrictive items of clothing (belt, tie, shoes) for the duration. If you practice meditation for at least 15 minutes twice a day, you will see immediate results. Whatever you believe yourself to be, you will eventually become, not only in your eyes but in the eyes of the world. It all begins in you and ends in you.

Mindfulness

Living in the moment, being present in the here and now, and mindful awareness. These are all examples of mindfulness. What exactly is mindfulness? What does it mean to be fully present in life? How can we go about living mindfully in our everyday lives when there are so many distractions, concerns and commitments directing our every waking moment? If you will allow me, I wish to guide you on a little journey of mindfulness.

To one degree or another, we all hold an awareness of our inner and outer world. Mindfulness, however, is a more focused sense of awareness. It is being aware of our living condition in the present moment.

Let us take a few minutes to explore being present in the here and now. Without judgment or desire to control anything, begin to become aware of your present state of being. Do not try to do or change anything; simply allow yourself be guided by the words you read here. Remain attentive, observant, and aware of your present state of being. Whenever you see ellipsis points (…), or symbol of continuation, take the time to fully explore the suggested area or sensation before reading further.

Now we begin.

Take three slow, deep breaths, feeling the air enter
your body, fill it and leave it...

Now bring mindfulness to your breath ...
where do you most sense your breath? ...
in your nose, your throat, your chest, your back,
your belly?...

Bring mindfulness to your breathing ...
its sound ... its rhythm ... its depth or
shallowness...its effect on your body...

Now bring mindfulness to your posture ...
are there areas of tension ... numbness ...
discomfort ...

Bring mindfulness to your toes ... feet ... legs ...
hips ... torso ... back ... arms ... hands ...
fingers ... neck ... throat ... head ... face ...
ears ... eyes ... mouth ... tongue ... nose ...

Return to your breath and be aware of it entering
and exiting your nostrils ...
what sensations are there? ...
does it feel warm, cool, dry, itchy, numb? ...

As you remain aware of the intimacy of your
breathing, continue to observe and listen.

Feel the weight of your body on the chair, couch,
floor or bed...

Feel the book in your hands ...
the texture of the paper ...

What do you hear around you? ...
    your breathing, the traffic, the radiator ...

What do you smell...?

What is the taste and texture like in your mouth...?

Look around you slowly and without naming or
    identifying anything, experience
    the colours ...
    the shape of objects ...
    the structure of the space ...
    the sensations of being alive in this place at this
    time ...

Now expand your awareness to include the other
    rooms ...
    then the whole building ...
    then, if you can, the entire block ...
    the city ...
    the country ...
    the continent ...
    the earth ...
    the universe ...

This is you in the here and the now, experiencing
the state of simply being alive in your present reality.

Metta: Loving Kindness

Metta is the meditation of love and kindness. It offers you the opportunity to develop and strengthen your inner intention of loving kindness towards yourself, towards all those who cross your path and towards every sentient being in the world.

Now that you find yourself more mindful of the present moment, with your body stiller and your mind calmer, it's the perfect moment to explore the profound nature of stillness and inner silence.

You're relaxed, your breath is slow and steady and you're sitting in a comfortable position. With each inhalation, imagine yourself being filled from the top of your head to the soles of your feet with a bright white or golden light. As this Divine light enters you it washes away all your cares, heals all your suffering and embraces your heart with soothing love. Then as you exhale, imagine that all your worries, fears, suffering and grief evaporating into nothingness. With each deepening breath, the light filling you becomes more luminescent, the love stronger.

Now say in your heart with conviction:
"I am filled with love,"
"I am filled with inner peace,"
"I am filled with compassion,"
"I am filled with joy,"
I am filled with equanimity,"
"I am filled with faith."

Say the previous sequence three times. Then say it again three times, but change the "I am filled" to

"May all beings be touched by my love…inner peace…"

Then do it three more times, saying,

"May all beings be filled with love… inner peace…"

When you have finished, send your loving intention out into the world. Return to your breath, take a few moments to let the feelings of loving kindness inhabit you, and then end with a thought, word or prayer of gratitude.

The abridged version—simply taking three long, deep breaths while saying "I am filled with love" before beginning an action: taking a call, opening your mail, eating a meal, beginning a presentation—bears immediate results. Each time you do this you'll find it easier to embrace your world with a loving smile.

21 Days of Smiles

At the beginning of part one, "A Hugger's Journey" I spoke of searching for a way out of the darkness that had engulfed me and the various means that I had explored to bring light back into my life. One method that stood out above the rest was a 21-day transformative journey. Every day for three weeks I went out into the world with the intention of bringing a little joy into my life by bringing a moment of sunshine into the life of a stranger.

Imagine that once a day for the next 21 days you will cheerfully greet or smile warmly to one stranger. At first it will feel awkward and even embarrassing, as the act of revealing yourself to others in such a spontaneous and genuine way is foreign to many of us. Be assured that if you persist, a deep feeling of joyful satisfaction will fill your heart each and every time you launch your beautiful smile at an unsuspecting stranger. The key is to smile or greet and continue on your way. Don't linger and expect a response. Like hugging, your gesture of goodwill has to be unconditional and free of attachments, otherwise it nullifies the gesture and the receiver may feel obliged to reciprocate. Let your kindness be your gift to an unsuspecting world and you will discover that, very quickly, your world has become everything that you've hoped it would be—a cheerful, caring, joyful place.

Sometimes it is good to end with a hug,

because every hug invites a new beginning!

PARTING WORDS

What a wonder we are, we humans, we beings of God, we children of the Earth. We are lost in our illusions of perfection, drowning in the sorrows of forgotten dreams and borrowed hopes—but we yearn for the knowledge that will reveal the gospel of our truth. We search everywhere, and yet what little we discover only leads us back to our beginnings. There is nothing beyond ourselves; all that is rests within our mighty little hearts. There, in that sacred place, resides all the wisdom, the comfort, the joy, the strength, the faith, the courage and the love that we need to sustain us during our journey.

Everyday life offers up countless opportunities to help us discover who we really are and what we can truly become. Each of us is unique, beautiful and true, as is every moment in our day. If only we would stop thinking about doing things and simply did what our hearts inspired us to, happiness might than find its way into our lives more often. To love or not to love, to be happy or not to be, to hug a life or to not—the choice is always ours to make. It is now, in this very moment, that you decide how your life will unfold tomorrow.

By touching the lives of others in a heartfelt way I have discovered a path towards happiness and fulfillment. This path I have shared with you in the hopes that you may discover your own way towards a joyful, meaningful and loving life, by sharing with others what you most desire yourself.

A heartfelt hug to you,

Martin Neufeld
The Hugger Busker